Roots and Wings

Five Generations and their Impact

D0293721

Roots and Wings

Five Generations and their Impact

ELIZABETH GOLDSMITH

OM
publishing

First published in 1998 by OM Publishing

04 03 02 01 00 99 98   7 6 5 4 3 2 1

OM Publishing is an imprint of Paternoster Publishing,
PO Box 300, Carlisle, Cumbria, CA3 0QS, UK
http://www.paternoster-publishing.com

British Library Cataloguing in Publication Data
A catalogue record for this book is available from the British Library

ISBN 1-85078-280-6

Cover Design by Mainstream, Lancaster
Typeset by WestKey Ltd, Falmouth, Cornwall
Printed in Great Britain by
Caledonian International Book Manufacturing Ltd, Glasgow

Contents

Abbreviations

ABCFM	American Board of Commissioners of Foreign Missions
ANCC	All Nations Christian College
CIM	China Inland Mission (later known as the OMF)
CMS	Church Missionary Society
IVF	Inter-Varsity Fellowship (later known as the UCCF)
OMF	Overseas Missionary Fellowship (now OMF International)
SCM	Student Christian Movement
SVM	Student Volunteer Movement
SVMU	Student Volunteer Missionary Union
UCCF	Universities and Colleges Christian Fellowship
WEC	Worldwide Evangelization Crusade (now WEC International)
YMCA	Young Men's Christian Association

Introduction

I was eleven years old when we returned to England. I remember standing on the deck of the old troopship, watching her slowly dock at Southampton, and wondering what my new life would be like. It was a cold December morning in 1945. The wind was gusting and the grey skies relentlessly discharged a steady drizzle.

Life had not been easy in China. The six of us children had been at a boarding school for missionaries' children together with several hundred other boys and girls. Our parents were scattered across hundreds of miles, engaged in their work, thankful that their offspring were receiving a 'good education'. But Japan invaded north China; and after Pearl Harbour our whole school was taken prisoner. For five years we were deprived of any family life – years when we had been cooped up with 1400 other people, with little to eat and inadequate heating and clothing. Our teachers valiantly attempted to continue our education. I had been allowed one exercise book in which I wrote out all my lessons in pencil and then rubbed them out and used the book again and again.

But for us as a family, the worst trauma hit us when word arrived that Mother had died, 1,000 miles away. I felt numb, not knowing how to grieve or cry. And during our last year of imprisonment none of our letters reached Father, so he had no sure knowledge of whether we were still alive.

When the war finally ended, Father eventually made his way out to the coast searching for us. It took him several months before we were re-united with him in Hong Kong. But he felt like a stranger, and relationships had to be painfully built up again.

Of course we were not the only children who suffered because of the war. What effect does a difficult upbringing have on any of us? Are we locked into our struggles, doomed to be handicapped by the bruising that life has thrown at us?

What about those who did not have loving parents as we six children did? Young people who have come from broken homes, or known verbal or physical abuse? What about those who are disadvantaged because of handicap, or poverty, or inadequate parental modelling? Are they trapped into repeating what they have learned? Or is there some way out?

I am a fourth generation missionary and have been researching my family tree to see what impact one generation has had on another. In our family we have all known hardship and suffering. Mistakes have been made and triumphs won. Each generation had exciting tales to tell of difficulties encountered and sacrifices made. Each generation made a significant contribution to the history of the Christian church and its mission. How did the task of mission develop over the years and what legacy did they pass on? In what way is the 'heritage' channelled within a family from one generation to another? And how is it modified and developed as new influences come in, often bringing new blessing?

Parents are like other people: we may all be daunted as we think of the defects in our own family line. Being human we are all flawed. One of the saddest features of western culture today is the number of broken marriages and thus of broken families. Both adults and children caught up in this cycle are likely to be burdened with negative feelings and an impaired self-image. They may well feel that their family line is seriously defective. No heritage is perfect, either in what we receive or in what we pass on. Much as we long to give the best to our children and to other young people around us, we never quite live up to our ideals. On the other hand, no heritage is completely disastrous. There will always be glimpses of unselfish love or loyalty or some other attractive quality, even in the most damaged environment.

And none of us is totally dependent on our upbringing. There seems to be a three-fold strand. Firstly, we inherit much from our forefathers. Secondly, we are shaped by our own generation and the values of society around us. But we are also all individuals, with freedom to choose what we will follow and what we will discard. Within one family, brought up in the same environment, the children may turn out very differently.

In addition, the influence which we exert on one another spreads more widely than our own immediate family. Some married couples have no children. Many people don't marry. Yet they can create a profound influence on others. So far as we know, the apostle Paul had no children. But he calls Titus 'my son in the faith' (1:4). Timothy also was Paul's son (1 Tim 1:1,2; 2 Tim 1:2). So was the escaped slave Onesimus (Phm v.10). It is true that Paul was presumably responsible, under God, for the conversion of each of these young men. But God has made all human beings in such a way that we do influence one another. And the Holy Spirit enhances this influence in a wonderful way.

I was discussing all this with my daughter the other day, thinking of the effect that people have on one another, and feeling the pain of so many who feel inadequate because of their past.

'But that's where Christ comes in!' Margaret retorted. 'Anyone can . . . START A NEW FAMILY LINE!'. I had burst in with the very same words she was using. The same thought gripped us both. We know so many people who are shackled by their inheritance and their surroundings. Families seem to be crumbling. Homes are breaking up. And the next generation wonders, 'How will I ever manage? What have I got to steady me, for me to cling onto? Am I going to be dragged into a life of unhappiness too?'

But the amazing thing is that, in Jesus Christ, the forces that drag people down and down in a sickening spiral can be overcome. The curse can be broken. By the power of the Holy Spirit anyone can make a new beginning, start a new family line. With a new beginning, we can pass on something of significance that will provide support and strength to face future challenges. Everyone has a part to play. We can all make a radical difference to those around us.

So maybe as I share a little of how God has blessed my family line, it can be an encouragement, even a symbol, to see the blessing God intends for his children. The Old Testament shows us a God who is bursting to bless, who longs to pour out a cascade of his blessing on those who will honour him. He planned it in strong family ties: parents who care for and support their children, children who honour their parents, fertile lands which produce abundant crops, laws which are just and equitable, and distribution of wealth such that all have enough and none become too rich or exploit the land. There was to be challenge too, and shouldering of new responsibilities, as they moved into a new country, developed the land and made full use of the resources God had provided.

God's same intention of blessing comes down to us today: families living together in harmony and security, and bringing the good news of Jesus Christ to a hurting world. God presents us with the stimulus of mutual challenge and development. And so a model was given for all generations, of families honouring God, being richly blessed by him, and sharing his blessing with the world around.

'Those who honour me I will honour' was one of my father's favourite verses from Scripture. And I have seen it clearly in his life – a life full of sacrifice (he lost all his possessions three times over in China) and yet full of blessing. This promise holds for all of us, married or single, widowed or divorced. So I have been prompted to trace the family line further back, beyond him and my mother to their parents and grandparents. In fact as far back as I can trace it.

This book is more than a family chronicle. In it I have tried to identify some different parts of the heritage that has been passed down and enriched through five generations of one family. I trust the story will be an encouragement to you, as it has been to me.

Elizabeth's Family Tree

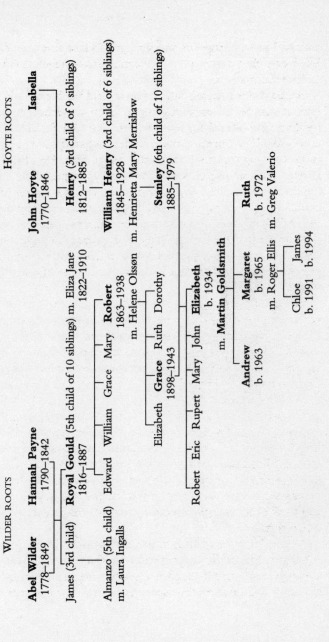

Chapter 1

Early Pioneers

The log cabin

Winters can be harsh in the far north of New York State, USA. The temperature will sometimes drop to thirty degrees below freezing. So an extra layer of mud sealed all the cracks in the log cabin where Royal Gould Wilder, my great-grandfather, was born in 1816. Often his father had to get up in the middle of the night and go to the shed where the cattle slept. Here he would crack his whip and chase them round and round until they got warm. Otherwise they would have frozen to death in their sleep!

Royal's parents had felled a small clearing in the woods to make a farm for themselves. Life on this border with Canada was rugged in the extreme. The reality of frontier living formed a sharp contrast to the stories told by Laura Ingalls Wilder, who years later married one of Royal's nephews. This was no cosy 'Little House on the Prairie', but an unceasing struggle to build a home from scratch and eke out a living on the edge of civilization.

Everything the Wilder family owned had to be made by themselves. Royal's mother would dye some wool with butter-nut shells. Then she would weave it, soak it, and shrink the cloth into heavy broadcloth. This she would make into trousers and coats so warm that the rain and cold could not penetrate. Her evenings would be spent knitting warm socks and mittens for the family. She made her own butter with milk from their cow, candles from the beef tallow and sugar from maple syrup in the spring. Her husband carved the yokes for the oxen himself and made the bob-sleds for them to pull piles of firewood over the snow. The family cut their own ice from the pond each winter when it had frozen solid; then stored it as huge ice-cubes, packed in sawdust, in the ice-house. Royal always looked forward to the treat of delicious ice-cream when the summer grew unbearably hot.

When his parents first cleared the land, the house they lived in had been a simple log cabin, made of hand-hewn logs, neatly fitted together. Over the years, as he had strength, Royal's father added some barns and extended the house. He had been trained as a ship's carpenter in his youth and later worked as a shoemaker before marrying, and so had the skill to turn his hand to anything. Royal soon learned that his father expected hard work and unquestioning obedience from his children. They were brought up to realize 'what you can't grow for yourself, or make for yourself, you can't have!' But on the other hand, almost anything necessary for basic living can be obtained if you set your mind to it, learn how it's made, and buckle to and produce it for yourself. So from a very young age Royal received a legacy of self sufficiency.

As the boys grew up, they also learnt complete independence. Their father planned what he wanted on his own farm, and no one was his master. Sheer will-power and determination enabled him to achieve his goals. The tenacity and capacity for hard work seen in Royal's later life probably came from his childhood training. He seems to have passed it on to his children too. But his independent spirit turned Royal into a loner, with strong ideas of his own. He found it hard to work in a team.

Royal and his brothers and sisters could go to school only in the winter when there was not so much pressing work on the farm. But he enjoyed his lessons and devoured every book he could find. Encouraged by his more educated mother, Royal would often study by the light of burning pine-knots late into the night. Eventually he was able to work his way through 'academy' (high-school) in Malone, five miles away.

During the year Royal was born there had been a spiritual revival in the area. Under godly men like Jonathan Edwards the movement known as 'The Great Awakening' had brought new life to the churches of New England in the previous generation. This was now spreading to the country areas, with a great emphasis on evangelism, especially because in the new colonies people were not automatically church members as they would have been in Europe before they migrated.

It is not known whether Royal's parents had shown any interest in religion previously. But as a result of the 1816 revival they began attending meetings. The Holy Spirit was working powerfully; and the young couple finally made their decision: they would trust in Christ as their Saviour and make him Lord of their little family and home. This was no mere passing fad. It changed their lives radically and brought a new set of priorities in the way they ran their farm.

So the momentous step was taken which would deeply affect future generations of my family. The legacy of a Christian heritage was beginning.

But as he grew up, Royal needed a personal faith in Christ. This came to him in a very striking way. One day, aged thirteen, he was sent through the woods to carry lunch to his father and brothers. Missing the way in the tangled undergrowth, he wandered around dazed and bewildered, and then realized he was continually coming back to the same place. Finding himself completely lost, he did not know which way to turn. In desperation he knelt down and prayed for guidance:

'O God, if you're really there, please help me!'

Struggling to his feet again, he determined to trust God to lead him. So he now walked purposefully forward, crying out to

God in his heart. After a short time he emerged from the wood right where his father and brothers were working! Relief and gratitude to God flooded his young heart, especially as 'panthers' (cougars) and wolves often roamed those parts!

Tied by the rigorous demands of his father's farm, Royal had to wait until he was twenty before he could fulfil his ambition and go to college. His strength and skills would be sadly missed as he left, but his parents did not stand in his way. They had little money to spare to help him with the fees, so he had been saving hard by cutting timber and selling it in the town. By sheer hard work he often hewed two 'cords' of wood a day: each a pile of six foot logs, stacked three feet high and lying seven feet along the ground. (Interestingly, when I visited my brother in Seattle some years ago, his son was earning his college fees in the same way, and proudly showed me his piles of neatly stacked logs.)

But even with these savings Royal had less than $10 when he set out, with his clothes and books tied in a bundle, to walk nearly a hundred miles to Middlebury College. A long lake lay between Malone and Middlebury. But he managed to earn his crossing by helping to load and unload the cargo of the ferry. Then setting off once more he carefully saved his shoes by walking barefoot most of the way!

Cutting hay in summer and splitting wood in winter, or doing whatever job came to hand, Royal was able eventually to work his way through college. He was never afraid of hard work, and the strength of his determination led him to graduate with honours. For the next four years he worked as a schoolmaster in Vermont. But God had other long-term plans for him. His spiritual life had been deepening all this time and he now faced a new challenge which would radically change his whole life. As he read Jonathan Edwards' *A History of the Work of Redemption*, God called him to give up his job and move into full-time Christian ministry. Being once more without a source of income as he began his training involved further sacrifice.

Preparation for Christian ministry

Andover Theological College, where Royal was now studying, had been founded as a protest against the liberal teaching which was creeping into Harvard University. The final straw came when a man who did not believe in the Trinity was appointed as Professor of Divinity. This was too much for those who based their theology on the Bible and saw what Jesus taught about Father, Son and Holy Spirit. Equally important to Royal's development, and the future of our family, was the fact that Andover was the place where the first American missionary society had been conceived.

As so often happens, this new development came through a group of young people who were open to God, and listening to his voice sufficiently closely to hear his longing for the world. These students started a secret club to pray for the vast areas of the world which had never heard the gospel. Meeting each week in the open-air, one day they were caught in a thunder storm and hurriedly took shelter by a haystack. As they continued their prayer and discussion in spite of the lashing rain, they became convinced God wanted them to pledge themselves for overseas mission. They called their band the 'Haystack Group' after that momentous day in 1810.

At Andover Seminary they were joined by several others, including Adoniram Judson who later (1812) became Burma's first Protestant missionary. His story is well worth reading for its challenge to sacrifice, as he suffered horrendously before he saw the beginning of the harvest with which God crowned his work. Judson and some others of the 'Haystack Group' walked the six miles to the annual meeting of their Congregational Church ministers. 'We have come to offer ourselves as missionaries to foreign lands,' they announced. 'Please advise us what to do, and how we can obey God's call.'

Their leaders were completely taken aback at this unexpected request. This was a totally new proposal. The idea of sending missionaries to other lands had never entered their heads! But as they thought and prayed about it they realized this was indeed the call of God. So the following day they set up the Board of Commissioners for Foreign Missions. In this way God used a small group of dedicated students to launch the American foreign missionary movement. It is amazing to think that today this comprises well over 60,000 missionaries, almost 70 per cent of the world-wide Protestant missionary force, and also contributes some 80 per cent of its finance!

As has happened so often, this working of the Holy Spirit in bringing revival through the Great Awakening led inexorably to the challenge for overseas mission. This is the same pattern as we see in Acts 1:8 – the power of the Holy Spirit was to be given primarily for one task: that the disciples might be witnesses in their own area (Jerusalem and Judea), to neighbouring people (Samaria) and on to the uttermost parts of the earth.

Meeting their successors at Andover College, Royal's horizons began to expand. He listened fascinated as men like Dr. Grant of Persia and Dr. John Scudder of India described their work. Eventually the feeling grew within him that the Lord was calling him too to this work.

But his class-mate from Middlebury College, who had graduated with equal honours, taunted him, 'Wilder, why *bury* yourself among the heathen?' With travel so hazardous in those days and medical knowledge so inadequate, becoming a missionary could be a costly business! It could well mean that you never saw your family again. Yet in the end this friend actually suffered more than Royal did. Rising rapidly in his profession as a lawyer, he married a lovely lady and became very wealthy. Sadly both his wife and their only daughter fell ill within a short time of each other and died. In his despair the poor man put a pistol to his head and shot himself.

Eliza Jane

While Royal had been teaching in Vermont he had become very attracted to one of his pupils, six years younger than himself. Dainty and petite, Eliza Jane Smith's slim build belied a strong character. But her grace and charm often won people over, whereas Royal's indomitable will could antagonize them. Eliza Jane had already been committed to overseas mission for several years. When she was a little girl, the story goes, someone came to the door collecting money for a missionary who was about to sail for the Sandwich Islands (as the Hawaiian islands were then known). Her mother's heart ached as she handed over a small coin. 'If only I could afford more!' she grieved to herself. The heavy feeling would not leave her all day. As she gathered her children for family prayers that evening she prayed aloud asking God to accept one or more of her children for missionary service. In telling the tale years afterwards Eliza Jane admitted, 'That prayer struck *me*. I knew I was to be the one!' And she gladly gave herself to God to serve him wherever he might send her.

When Royal first met Eliza Jane she was living with her saintly grandfather in West Rutland, Vermont, as there was no 'academy' near her home. Years later she loved to tell her children of the lasting impression made on her by her grandfather's faithful attendance at the Tuesday night prayer meeting at the school house. 'One night a great storm let loose and the ground was covered with sleet. Grandpa was so old we were afraid he might slip and fall on the ice. So we begged him not to go. But it was the meeting to pray for the Holy Spirit, so he would not listen to us. He went, and then was very late getting home. We thought it was such a dreadful night, that surely no one else had gone. We asked him, "Well Grandpa, who came out this evening?" Peacefully he answered, "God was there, and our meeting was very blessed – alone with God." '

It is interesting to note that there was strong desire for the Holy Spirit already in those days.

So while Royal studied at Andover Theological College, Eliza Jane attended an all-ladies' seminary called Mount Holyoke. They were married in March 1846; and a mere six months later sailed for Bombay under the American Board of Commissioners for Foreign Missions. They had little idea of what life would be like in India, or whether they would ever return home again. But they had taken Jesus Christ not only as Saviour but also as Lord, and so were willing to make any sacrifice for him.

Their extraordinary courage and faith in leaving America challenged many people at their farewell meeting. Several gave their lives to Christ as a result. So the Spirit-directed movement of revival leading to mission now completed its natural circle: obedience to mission led to further revival. God longs to move us all into this cycle of blessing.

To India

It was to be 120 days before they could stretch their legs on dry land again. With another young missionary couple on board, their cargo ship crossed the Atlantic, rounded the Cape of Good Hope, and battled on. At times they were exposed to squalls and even hurricanes and at other times experienced monotonous calms. Their diet grew increasingly inadequate, and there was always the fear that lack of vitamin C would lead to scurvy, the 'sailors' curse'. But the little team of four held services on deck, cared for any sailors who were ill, and pressed on with the study of the Marathi language which they had already started three months earlier. Royal wrote to his father, 'Among my deficiencies as a missionary, I trust a neglect to master the language will not be one.'

Royal's diligence in language learning showed itself in an incident which happened only three months after their arrival. His senior missionary had to be away one Sunday. 'How about you preaching instead?' he enquired with a twinkle in his eye. It was meant as a joke. But Royal rose to the challenge and preached his first sermon in Marathi. The national Christians were amazed; but some said simply, 'We prayed for him!'

The land to which Eliza Jane and Royal had travelled was a huge subcontinent, teeming with millions of people. Hundreds and thousands of villages were scattered across its vast expanse. Very few of them had even heard of Christianity, let alone listened to the gospel. It was a country of geographical extremes, with the lofty Himalayas to the north, the wide Gangetic plains to the north-east and extensive deserts towards the north-west. A high north-south ridge of mountains formed a sharp escarpment on the western side, dropping down more gradually to the eastern shores. Ahmednagar, where they were to spend their first six years, was situated on this sloping eastward side of the Western Ghats, 175 miles north-east of Bombay.

The Indian peoples had inherited a rich, ancient civilization, stretching back for centuries. Many ornate temples and palaces dotted the landscape. The beautiful mausoleum of the Taj Mahal had already stood for two hundred years. A large proportion of the population followed Hinduism with its profound philosophies and its thousands of gods and exotic ancient myths and legends. Others were Muslims, Sikhs, or Jains. All held strongly to their own beliefs. It was not going to be easy to show that Christianity had anything to offer.

But Protestant missionary work had recently begun. The great pioneer William Carey, who served forty years in Bengal, hundreds of miles to the east, had died a mere twelve years before the Wilders arrived. His initial work had been made extremely difficult by the East India Company which controlled most of that vast area, and jealously guarded the trading rights. They feared anything which might interfere with their business and profits. So the trio, Carey, Marshman and Ward, had been forced to find refuge in the Danish settlement. But the Evangelicals in England, who had a strong voice in Parliament, had been pressing for the opening of India without restriction to missionary work. By the time Royal and Eliza Jane arrived this had been achieved. They must have felt deeply grateful to dedicated Christians who as high-ranking politicians had been able to influence the laws.

The young couple greatly admired the ministry of Alexander Duff. He had started work in Calcutta on the east coast of India some ten years earlier. Rather than concentrating solely on evangelism, Duff's vision was to focus on education. Through it he hoped to reach the upper classes who would be strategic to the spread and development of Christianity throughout the country in the future. Explaining his strategy in penetrating the formidable fortress of Hinduism, Duff stated: 'While you engage indirectly separating as many precious atoms from the mass as the stubborn resistance to ordinary appliances can admit, we shall, with God's blessing, devote our time and strength to the preparing of a mine . . . which shall one day explode and tear up the whole from its lowest depths' (George Smith, *The Life of Alexander Duff*: London 1881). Starting from a group of only five boys, his school quickly grew to two hundred. But the Hindu leaders reacted violently when four young men were converted. The disturbance nearly forced the school to close. But he persevered, and from his converts came founders of some of today's most notable Indian Christian families.

The missionaries in Ahmednagar had a similar vision for education. Royal's academic bent was quickly noticed by his senior missionary and he was soon put in charge of their mission's school of 70–80 boys. He warmed to this task, feeling it could be the key to winning the local population for Christ. Education would enable them to read the Bible for themselves and be trained to teach others. So he concentrated on setting up new schools. Within a year six city schools had been established, and within three years twenty more village schools which would feed into the central schools. The Wilders, horrified to discover that the earlier missionaries had actually paid a small fee to each pupil, thinking this was the only way they would be willing to attend, abolished the practice. Much to their relief, nobody objected. In fact many people were beginning to see the advantage of education, and even more boys enrolled.

Kolhapur

The neighbouring Native State of Kolhapur, 200 miles south of Ahmednagar, had never been evangelized and was almost unexplored by missionaries. For some years the Wilders' missionary society had been wondering about starting work there. So in 1852 with six years' experience behind them and a good grasp of the language, Royal and Eliza Jane were asked to move to the capital city and begin evangelism there.

The task they faced was to prove extremely difficult. Having obtained a letter stating that the Government had 'no objection' to their starting work there, they promptly set out. But by local brahmins (the Hindu priestly caste) Kolhapur was considered, next to Benares (known today as Varanasi), to be the holiest city on earth. No foreigners were allowed to contaminate it by their presence, let alone those seeking to win the local people over to a foreign religion. The brahmins immediately petitioned that they be banished from the State. No local person was willing to give the Wilders shelter, or even to speak to them. Anyone who had anything to do with them would be considered ceremonially defiled.

What this must have meant to the young couple can only be imagined. A less dedicated pair might easily have given up after a few months. How they managed is not related, but after some time they were able to find shelter in an old house in an army camp. But still the hostile looks and the angry words which followed them everywhere made them feel very vulnerable.

In answer to the Wilders' petition, the Bombay Government eventually notified the Maharaja that 'Christian missionaries must be accorded the same rights in the State as were given to the members of other religions . . . but they need not listen to the missionaries' preaching.'

The high-handed way in which the British Government overruled the feelings of the local leaders did not make things any easier for the Wilders; but at least they now knew they would not be thrown out! But how were they to gain a hearing, when everyone around had been warned against even speaking to them? This was the question they prayed over. Gradually Royal and Eliza Jane's plans came back to what they had been doing previously – starting schools.

Enquiries revealed only one school of twelve boys in a back street, and that in a city of 44,000 people. So as soon as they were able to rent a house Royal announced that he would open a school. Again the brahmins were furious. They complained to the Maharaja that he must be stopped. But the Maharaja's sister, Akasahib, the 'power behind the throne', was intrigued by the foreigners and enquired closely about what they were doing. Instead of closing the school, she sent boys from the palace to attend it! So Royal and Eliza Jane continued to find themselves the centre of controversy. A few people were curious to know what they were doing, and even willing to send their children to learn to read and write. But many proved extremely antagonistic, and made life as difficult as they could.

A contemporary of Royal Wilder describes him as 'a man of inflexible will . . . He never chose the easy way, but faced difficulties with victorious courage and dauntless hope. He was a man to admire rather than to love.' Such strength of character was certainly needed to sustain him through these difficult days. We have seen how as a young man he had learnt to surmount huge difficulties, and the present situation only strengthened his determination not to give up.

As I look at my photos of Eliza Jane I wonder what sort of person she was. She has a gentle face with a kind expression, but a firm set to her mouth. She is always dressed in western clothes,

with a high collar and long sleeves, which she must have found
almost unbearably hot in the tropical weather. Did she envy the
local ladies their cool saris with their beautiful colours? Missionaries in China at this time were afflicted with terrible prickly heat
because of the western style clothes they wore. Some could not
sleep for the irritation; and spots that were scratched became septic.

During her time in India Eliza Jane had to face many dangers:
snakes in the house, a scorpion on her son's coat, a panther
crossing her path while out for a walk and rioting mobs who
hurled a stone through the window right across her daughter's
cradle. Eliza Jane had no other western woman to be a companion to her – no one in whom she could confide and with whom
she could share her hopes and fears, except her determined
husband. They were the only missionaries among four million
people. William Carey's wife found a similar situation too much
for her and went out of her mind. It says much for Eliza Jane's
and Royal's commitment to each other and to the Lord and the
high calling he had given them, that they kept going.

Gradually the number of pupils increased, and some of the
parents began attending with their children, so that the rented
house became too crowded. As they continued to pray about the
many obstacles, the hostile feeling against them must have eased
a little because Royal began to negotiate to buy some land on
which to build a school. The senior Secretary of the American
Board, Dr. Rufus Anderson, had advised him against purchasing
land. 'Wait and see if you can hold on' had been the instructions.
But Royal and Eliza Jane never doubted that they could, and
would, hold on.

Using their own money, they were eventually able to buy a
piece of land with two small huts on it. While running the school
in these temporary buildings, Royal began to erect what they
longed for – a simple church, 15 by 10 metres, which could be
used for worship on Sundays and serve as a school at other times.
Royal himself helped to quarry the stone, and supervised every
stage of the project, nailing on each of the roof tiles with his own

hand. How thankful he must have been for his upbringing on a farm!

The opposition from the local brahmins still continued, but the mission school now began to blossom. Education became increasingly valued by the local community. More people, adults as well as children, began to attend. Then Eliza Jane took the much more daring step of opening a school for girls in the bazaar the following year. Much to her joy, the Maharaja's sister encouraged her in this, even though up to that time an educated woman was considered a disgrace in India. 'What, a girl learn to read!' someone exclaimed. 'If a buffalo can be taught, then I'll believe a girl can learn!'

But Eliza Jane was not to be daunted. She had a strong conviction that she had been called to missionary work in her own right, and saw this as her vital contribution to their work. By her winsomeness and perseverance she was able to win through, and her girls' school prospered. This little school which Eliza Jane opened in Kohlapur bazaar in 1853 gradually developed into the Esther Patton School, which has had a long and noble history. However Eliza Jane's and Royal's other great desire was still unfulfilled. For the first four years no one was willing to take the step of following Christ. So as the schools grew in size they were forced to employ non-Christian teachers, while still attempting in every way to make the gospel clear.

These schools gave the Wilders the opportunity they longed for, because through them they could give Christian instruction alongside the other subjects. All pupils learned by heart the Lord's Prayer, the Ten Commandments, the Catechism and hymns, and they listened frequently to a clear presentation of the gospel.

Rufus Anderson

It is against this background that the bombshell of Dr. Rufus Anderson's visit to India in 1855 must be understood. As a young man Anderson had volunteered for overseas mission; but with his organizational gifts and clear thinking he had been kept back to work on the home staff of the American Board. Twenty years older than Royal Wilder and with the role of senior Secretary, he carried a great deal of authority in the mission and is today recognized as one of the great missionary statesmen of the nineteenth century.

Rufus Anderson and several like-minded men became keenly aware that the strategy of missions had not been clearly thought through. When the American Board had started work a generation earlier among the American Indians and the Hawaiians, they had not stopped to consider the theory behind their work. Their task seemed obvious: the world needed to be evangelized, and this they would do by bringing them the gospel. But unconsciously they associated evangelism with western civilization. After all, hadn't God blessed the western way of life? And weren't its values based on the Bible? Education was seen as the key means of 'civilizing the natives', and so hopefully making people more open to receive the gospel message. However, the results of this early work had been meagre; so a complete change of policy was called for.

Anderson and the other members of the Board felt that the goal of mission must be clarified. Once that was clear, everything else must be subordinated to this target. With typical western individualism, Anderson insisted that the 'simple and sublime' aim of every mission was the conversion of individuals through the preaching of the gospel. He wrote, 'Missions are instituted for the spread of a scriptural, self-propagating Christianity. This is their only aim.'

Anderson considered that this could be done by:

'1. the conversion of lost men
2. organizing them into churches
3. giving these churches a competent native ministry
4. conducting them to the stage of independence and (in most cases) of self propagation.'

This constituted a remarkable progress in mission thinking. Now at last mission leaders were giving careful thought to their strategy. But the implications of these ideas need to be clearly understood.

In focusing the missionaries' task on this one clear aim, Anderson stated that all other 'auxiliary' means had to be kept strictly subordinate to preaching. Bible translation, literature, schools and any other activities were secondary. In restricting the missionary task to that of evangelism, Anderson stipulated that missionaries should move on as soon as possible, leaving the local church under 'native pastors who should be given full Christian liberty to manage their own affairs'. This worthy desire that 'native' churches should be allowed to develop freely meant the English-medium schools were frowned upon, as they automatically introduced a foreign element.

On his arrival in India, Rufus Anderson flatly forbade the use of English-medium schools. However, just before his arrival the team of missionaries had agreed to start an English-medium school in Bombay, since English was now the official language of administration. Such a school would provide wide opportunities for its graduates, both in further theological studies and in government employment. It could become a great attraction to draw future leaders under the sound of the gospel. So this new directive was greeted with dismay.

Anderson also refused to allow non-Christian teachers to be employed in the mission schools. He felt this set a wrong precedent. This too was a harsh blow to missionaries like Royal Wilder. At that time there were no Christians he could employ in Kolhapur. If he and Eliza Jane were to teach more than a handful of people, they would need to employ non-Christians to help them.

It seemed inevitable that Anderson and Wilder would clash. The strong-minded Anderson has been charged with being 'a tyrant who ruled the missionaries with an iron hand'. Someone has described Royal Wilder as 'over-bearing and headstrong'. Anderson vehemently stressed the logic of his new strategy, while Wilder felt the missionaries were being pressurized into acquiescing against their own judgment. He was horrified to see his colleagues begin to change their minds. He demanded to see

evidence that preaching had been more successful than education, and quoted his own difficult experience when everyone
had refused to speak to the missionary couple, until finally they
were able to offer something which the local people wanted.
They had to find a key to open people's hearts.

This was a classic example of two strong-minded men, coming
from completely different backgrounds, and with different experiences of life, clashing profoundly in their views and refusing to
entertain the idea that the other person might have some right
on their side.

Reading about this conflict reminded me that specific life
situations often challenge us to reconsider our theories. People
cannot be put into boxes. They are the varied and often surprising
creation of Almighty God. Interestingly, within a few years
Anderson's view of English-medium schools was reversed. People soon saw what a valuable contribution these Christian schools
could give.

This head-on clash with their mission leaders created a very
difficult atmosphere. Sadly, Royal and Eliza Jane's sense of injury
and injustice seems to have grown. As other missionaries were also
dissatisfied, the American Board appointed a committee to examine Anderson's Deputation. Voluminous letters were sent back
and forth, mostly deeply critical. Royal objected to the dictatorial
attitude of the Deputation; and together with other Presbyterian
and Reformed missionaries, he was unwilling to allow the 'native'
churches to develop freely in their own style. Steeped as they were
in their own denominational forms, the missionaries felt their own
forms of worship were the truest expression of Christianity.

Royal's initial broadside consisted of a 34-page document to
the Home Council! He followed this with letters to newspapers
and journals in Bombay, Calcutta and New York, charging his
fellow missionaries with cowardly acquiescence to the
domineering Anderson. A full-scale battle had now broken out.

It was probably at this point in his life that an incident occurred
which was later described by Rev. John Wright, for 32 years a

missionary in Persia (Iran), who heard it from Royal Wilder in 1877 when Wright was a student at Princeton University. Utterly discouraged at the attitude of the Board, Royal and Eliza Jane decided there was nothing for it but to give up and go home. Dejectedly they sold all their household goods except for a few essentials. Packing up what remained, Royal, Eliza Jane and their two children set off in an ox cart for the long journey home. A hot bumpy ride lay ahead of them. Their hearts were heavy at the thought of what was driving them away – not the difficulty of the work, or the opposition of the brahmins, but a deep disagreement with their own leaders.

After a while they came to a swollen river. Royal was used to such obstacles from his childhood days. After surveying the river carefully, he began to cross at what looked like a shallow place. But disaster struck, as the wheels stuck in midstream. With the water swirling round them, and the children clinging to their mother, he could not get the cart to move, however hard he tried.

Suddenly they heard voices on the opposite bank and, looking up, they saw a cavalcade of British officers, led by Sir Henry Bartle Frere, who later became Chief Commissioner of Sind and was subsequently appointed Governor of Bombay (1862–7). Having sent to enquire about the Europeans who were marooned in the river, and being told they were a missionary family returning to America, he ordered some of his men to help them out of their desperate situation and asked why they were leaving. Hearing of their frustrated hopes, he urged them not to give up. 'Go back to your work in Kolhapur', he said, 'and open your schools again. India needs you, and them. I promise to be personally responsible for all expenses.'

Royal and Eliza Jane were so impressed by his generosity that they did return. Wright concluded his story: 'Sir Bartle Frere fulfilled to the letter his assurance of support. As long as the Wilders were able to stay in India he provided liberally for them, and for the educational and evangelistic work which they engaged in.'

Additional Note to Chapter 1

How can the controversy between Royal Wilder and Rufus Anderson be evaluated today? Several important aspects emerge:

1. This situation can easily arise when a committee, far removed from the locality, seeks to propound theories and draw up guidelines. The reasons for doing so may be correct, since often the people on the spot are so totally immersed in their work that they fail to grasp the overall view. On the other hand, they know the local situation well. At that very time, Hudson Taylor, in far-off China, was growing increasingly frustrated at working under mission leaders based in London who had little real knowledge of his local conditions or of his work. Within the next decade he had founded a mission whose head-quarters would be on the 'field' and not in the sending country.

This danger can recur today. I still notice western churches wanting to determine what their missionaries do in overseas situations about which they have little intimate knowledge. This can create severe problems.

2. This disagreement clearly shows the importance of being willing to listen to other people. Listening must take place in an attitude of openness while trying to understand the other person's point of view. Both Anderson and Wilder had good and genuine reasons for their stance. Both viewpoints should have been recognized, and then woven into the final outcome of their discussions.

3. While recognizing that it can be helpful to clarify goals, Anderson appears to have had too simplistic a view of mission. The preaching of the gospel is certainly important, but worldwide mission is not limited merely to preaching. Our Lord's final words in the Great Commission of Matthew 28:18–20 clearly

say we are to go into all the world and preach the gospel. But an intrinsic part of the task he gave us was to 'teach them to observe all that I have commanded you'. Paul's example in Acts demonstrates that teaching the new converts and pastoring them was very much the task of mission, as well as training local people to teach and pastor. He went far beyond the initial preaching.

4. Holistic mission is much emphasized today because it is realized that people are not just 'souls' needing to be saved, but whole persons with physical, emotional, and mental needs as well as spiritual ones. For many years, schools as well as other professional activities such as medicine, agriculture and development work were looked on as a means to an end; they were a useful bait to attract people to listen to the preaching. More recently, however, it has been realized that mission is two-pronged, involving both word-based and community-based evangelism. Both are an integral part of the task we have been given. This means that education has a validity in itself and is not just a means to an end.

Anderson does not stand alone in unduly simplistic approaches to mission. In our day it is easy to allow slogans such as 'church growth', 'unreached peoples', 'the 10/40 window' and 'missionary bonding' to restrict our vision and force us into forms of mission which may not be appropriate. These catchy phrases often have a positive role in stimulating missionary concern, but, as with Anderson, they do not reflect the fullness of the biblical task of mission.

5. In his desire to see clear results and focus on priorities, Anderson seems to have failed to realize that different members of his mission would have different gifts. Some no doubt could walk the streets of India, preach the gospel, and hope to see results. But others needed to use their different gifts in the extension of the kingdom. All members should be encouraged to develop their strong points, while at the same time considering

how they fit into the team as a whole. The great variety of talents which God has showered on his people should be used to the full. Leaders must not attempt to squeeze everyone into the same mould.

6. The goal of mission which Rufus Anderson was propounding led within a few years to the well-known formula that churches founded through mission are to be encouraged to become self-governing, self-supporting and self-propagating; and this has been regarded as a worthy ideal in many countries. However, the desire to encourage young churches to stand on their own feet has not always been easy to achieve. Of course it is true that if the missionary stays too long the local church may be stifled. But if the change-over to national leadership is too rapid the young church may founder and stagnate, as its members are not sufficiently mature to carry such responsibility.

Stephen Neill gives an example of this in his *History of Christian Mission* (Penguin Books, Harmondsworth, 1986). In 1860, only five years after Royal's disagreement with Anderson, a 'Native Pastorate' was established in Sierra Leone and all missionaries were withdrawn. But the leaders were not ready for this responsibility, and Neill comments, 'This inflicted on the Church a paralysis from which a whole century did not avail to deliver it' (p. 221). The Overseas Missionary Fellowship also tried out this policy in the 'new villages' of Malaysia in the 1950s. Their ex-China workers tried to withdraw as soon as possible from two of their centres. But the new converts were too weak in the faith to cope. Many of the gifted nationals had moved into the towns, and those who remained had little leadership ability.

7. Anderson appears to distinguish sharply between Church and Mission. But Neill points out that 'any such sharp separation between Church and Mission . . . seems to lack theological foundation in the New Testament'. Indeed, the emerging churches need to be taught to become mission centres themselves

and reach out into their own community and beyond. Acting as a 'partner in mission', the missionary's task is to model what it means to have a mission vision. Working alongside the local leaders, they can train others accordingly. As the Bible clearly demonstrates, evangelistic mission should form an intrinsic part of the life and structures of the local church. This is a very topical issue today with which British and other European churches must grapple.

8. As many others have done, Anderson looked to the record of Paul's missionary journeys as his model for planning his own strategy. He summarized his thoughts in his book, *Foreign Missions: their relations and claims*. While noting Paul's evangelistic thrust, Anderson found no record of any aim to transform society as a whole. This was what led him to oppose efforts to 'civilize' the natives, but rather to concentrate on preaching.

But we need to ask, 'Is the New Testament account a blueprint for all activities of the church down the ages? Or is it intended to supply principles? If we cannot find a particular method of working in Scripture, does that mean we should not adopt it? In reality it is clear that all present-day churches use many approaches which we cannot find in the Bible: Sunday Schools, women's meetings, birthday parties, to name but a few. The Bible is given us to clarify principles of working, not to cramp our ideas. Royal was quite right to feel that mission schools were in line with the spirit of Christ, as long as his aim in founding them was to promote Christ's kingdom in Indian society.

9. In their desire to start an English-medium school, the Wilders and their fellow missionaries had glimpsed an enormous potential. The knowledge of English would bring tremendous advantages both in educational progress and in new openings for employment, as well as enabling deeper spiritual growth through the wide selection of books which could now be read. Of course Anderson's emphasis on vernacular schools was also important. Such schools

did not impose a foreign culture, but acknowledged the validity of the local language and cultural expression. They also met people's immediate needs. Both partners in the dispute had validity in their arguments. Missionaries often walk a tight-rope in this area of language. The use of national languages encourages indigenization, but can eventually be seen as continuing tribal divisions. It can therefore be divisive. National governments sometimes level this accusation today at the Wycliffe Bible Translators, as their work appears to emphasize the divisions within a country rather than the national unity. And yet it is true that people need the Scriptures in their own 'heart language'.

Within a few years Anderson's view on English-medium schools was reversed. Today the contribution which these Christian schools have made to the development of the church in India can be clearly seen. In spite of fifty years of freedom from colonial power, English is still one of the unifying languages of that country. It also opens the door to wider international relationships.

10. Lastly, as the missionary on the spot, Wilder knew the local situation well. He was not just concerned with mission theories, but with living people. He knew them personally and was concerned with their needs. It was obvious to him that education was something that would help them. Also in his situation he had no other option. For months no one had been willing to speak to him until he was able to offer them something they wanted. He had to find the key to open their hearts.

Chapter 2

Never Give Up

The bitter antagonism which the Wilders had met from the Kolhapur brahmins proved to be part of a much wider animosity which was seething under the surface. For too long India had been subjected to the exploitative schemes of the East India Company, whose open purpose for remaining was to make as much financial profit as possible. Of course there was right and wrong on both sides, but 1857, the year of the Indian Mutiny, has been described as a date forever etched on the history of British dealings with India. Wild rumours were circulating that, through the efforts of the foreign missionaries, there were plans forcibly to convert the whole population to Christianity.

The unexpected explosion of the Indian Mutiny struck all things 'western' with devastating fury. Most of the Indian troops in the British army mutinied and tried to assassinate their British officers. In Kolhapur three officers were murdered in their homes. The rest fled for refuge to the Residency, passing a night of terror in imminent danger of their lives. In various places throughout India missionaries and chaplains were killed, while not even their little children were spared. As the news broke upon the western world it was greeted with shock and horror.

But by God's loving grace, on that very day in May 1857, the Wilder family were boarding a sailing ship in Bombay harbour to return to America. A severe attack of cholera some months previously had left Royal so weak that his doctor advised a return home to build up his strength. Doggedly he clung on, but eventually he had to give in. Surely the Lord allowed his continuing weakness as a protection against what was about to happen. They were reluctant to leave because they had just baptised their first two converts. They also knew it would mean closing their schools temporarily, and five hundred children would suffer. But they hoped to return as soon as they were fit again.

A year passed happily in the more bracing climate of New England and once more Royal felt well enough to go back to India. He wrote to his mission to express their readiness now to resume work in Kolhapur, but was shocked to receive a discouraging reply after some weeks. At their annual meeting the previous day the Board had voted to discontinue the Kolhapur mission! The Wilders knew there would be no opportunity to appeal until the next annual meeting. Something was badly wrong, but little could be done about it. Clearly the earlier misunderstandings had not yet been resolved.

But Royal and Eliza Jane were not ones to give up easily. They tried again the following year, only to be told very bluntly this time that the Kolhapur mission was definitely closed. Furthermore the collections for Kolhapur they had been taking up at their meetings had not been sanctioned by Dr. Anderson! A researcher into these events writes:

'The struggle which followed far surpassed Wilder's participation in the Deputation controversy. Rufus Anderson warned the Prudential Committee that "we must make up our minds to meet, in him, the most difficult returned missionary, perhaps, that we have had to deal with". The Wilders' case dragged on for a year and a half, until they were finally dismissed by the Board in the spring of 1860.'

Royal felt deeply humiliated and seethed with anger. Apparently only one member of the whole committee was willing to meet him face to face. And, with careless disregard for a missionary's rights, this man stated that, 'the Prudential Committee has the same right to dismiss a missionary as an employer has to dismiss a disliked clerk'. Such a remark was hardly likely to

improve matters! However Royal laid the blame chiefly on
Anderson himself. Royal's strong feelings of injustice seem to
have made him more sure than ever of his own opinion. He gives
the impression of being a man of inflexible will, convinced that
there was little or no room for any other view than his own. He
actually had very good and quick judgment; he could summarize
a situation very rapidly, and almost immediately sense the best
course of action. However he did not, and could not, make many
friends, and seldom drew others into his confidence and planning.
According to one source: 'He disclosed his plans to his associates
only through work accomplished.'

We may ask, what kind of father would this determined man
be to his children? None of the accounts mentions his family
relationships until he was much older. Would his children inherit
his inflexibility and capacity to antagonize others? Would they
be as self-opinionated as he? Or would such a strong father repress
the development of his children, leaving them withdrawn and
unsure of themselves? And what about their mother? Did she
have some softening traits which would help to offset her
husband's crustiness?

We shall find the answers to these questions as the family story
unfolds.

Western denominations

Royal and Eliza Jane had now reached the point where they
realized they must look for a different mission board under
which to work. The American Board of Foreign Missions had
been set up as an ecumenical venture, with a variety of different
denominations working together. But by 1850 many Presbyterian members were having second thoughts. They felt that the
freedom Anderson was offering to the emerging churches was
detrimental to the spread of biblical Reformed Christianity
throughout the world. So there was strong pressure for a more

explicitly Presbyterian mission with the aim of establishing 'foreign presbyteries' with the same church order, worship forms and doctrine as the 'mother church'. This was in line with the Wilders' own feelings. They now appealed to their home presbytery to send them out to Kolhapur and support them. Much to their relief, the presbytery eventually expressed full confidence in them with only a small minority dissenting, and formed a committee to sponsor an independent mission in Kolhapur.

Was this a backward step? Were my great-grandparents right to move from an ecumenical mission expressing Christian unity in Christ and join one solely under their own denomination? As a result they moved their fledgling church into the arms of a western denomination. Was not this type of action merely exporting our western divisions, and failing to demonstrate that oneness in Christ which was at the centre of our Lord's prayer in John 17?

My great-grandparents had little choice, as this was the only door open to them in 1860. Things were different in 1960 when I was a new candidate with the Overseas Missionary Fellowship. As a convinced Anglican I was urged to join their 'Anglican field' in North Malaya. I demurred, since my sincere but naive desire was to avoid exporting my own denomination, but rather to give the national churches freedom to develop as they desired. However, I found myself working, first in a Reformed Presbyterian church in Indonesia, then in a Brethren assembly in Malaysia which was seeking to join the Presbyterians, and later in a Life Bible Presbyterian church in Singapore. Before all that I had worshipped briefly in the Anglican cathedral!

Even in 1960 I could not get away from western denominations! I had not at that point appreciated the practicalities of the situation. Before a new church is fully formed, the enquirers and then the converts are watching their missionaries closely. Many questions are in their minds. How do Christians worship? How do they pray? How do they make decisions? What sort of

leadership structures do they follow? In answering these and
many other questions the local missionaries cannot help but act
as models; and naturally they model what they know already. It
would be very difficult for the new believers to create a church
which spurned these role-models from the beginning and fully
followed indigenous patterns. For instance, what would be an
indigenous form of prayer, if the only prayer familiar to new
Christians was the offerings performed in a Hindu temple? What
does it mean for the church to be 'the body of Christ' when the
previous forms of religion were very individualistic and they had
no corporate services?

In my experience, where interdenominational missions plant
churches these often follow the lowest common denominator
i.e. those aspects of Christian faith and life which all can agree
on. They often turn out to have a 'congregational' structure,
where each local church is autonomous and only loosely linked
with the others. The worship will probably be non-liturgical and
often non-charismatic, supposedly 'free' but quickly conforming
to its own tight patterns. It is true that denominational churches
can carry overtones of imperialism, but there is no need for the
daughter churches to cling rigidly to the structures they were
given. Today several Anglican churches planted by such missions
as the South American Missionary Society demonstrate how
flexible and varied a denominational church can be. Looking
further afield, the advantages of belonging to a world-wide
organization are enormous.

But it was still early days for Protestant missions when my
great-grandparents were planning to return to India. The various theories had not yet been tested out. Happily, a century
later, India led the way in seeking to demonstrate Christian
unity. After 28 years of difficult negotiation and hard work, the
Church of South India was set up in 1947, linking Anglicans,
Methodists, Presbyterians, Congregationalists and Basel Mission
(Swiss and German). How they managed to establish a basis of
unity between such widely differing denominations is well

worth studying. Today the Evangelical Fellowship of India links together many churches and agencies. It has made a significant impact on the church, backing the strategic Union Bible Seminary at Pune, and providing much useful support through pastors' retreats, literature production, Sunday School courses and Theological Education by Extension.

Before returning to India, Royal Wilder published *Mission Schools in India*, in which he presented a detailed history and defence of their schools, demonstrating that every convert of good caste had been brought to Christ through the schools. Was it his final act of defiance as he sailed? Someone commented that 'it was full of himself and his work'. But the *Presbyterian Quarterly Review* supported him in their comparative review of Wilder's book and Anderson's *Memorial Volume of the First Fifty Years of the ABCFM*.

The years at home had brought Royal and Eliza Jane a deep sorrow and a great joy. One young daughter had died and little Grace had been born. Now they faced the further pain of leaving their eldest son Edward behind for his education. They were not to see him again for eight years. Their first term of service in India had been more than ten years. The suffering created by lengthy partings from loved ones was very painful in those days when travel was difficult and telephones had not yet been invented.

The Church in Kolhapur

Arriving back at last in Kolhapur in 1861, the Wilders were shocked to discover that their church had been sold over their heads by order of the American Board. They had not even been informed. To add insult to injury, it had been bought by some Muslims and converted into a mosque! Full of indignation, Royal called on Major Havelock, the British Resident (i.e. Government Agent), and showed him the title deeds. Havelock tried to placate him with the offer of another site; and over the

months various places were suggested. Finally Royal admitted
which site he was gunning for – right next door to the former
church! This was not the most tactful place to suggest –
especially when it transpired that it was the Maharaja's wrestling
pit. Major Havelock told him it was out of the question.

But with his usual dogged determination to get his own way,
Royal appealed to Sir Bartle Frere, now Governor of Bombay.
Very generously he reimbursed Wilder for the loss of the church
and sent him a substantial contribution for his work. How it
happened we do not know, but within a year Royal was able to
purchase the site he wanted and began to erect another church.
Much annoyed at Royal's high-handed behaviour, the Resident
tried to have the sale declared illegal; and the Muslims presented
a petition attempting to prohibit the building of a church next
to their mosque. But Royal stubbornly stuck to his purpose, and
somehow managed to persuade the Maharaja to contribute the
long beams required for building the church from his own estate.
Royal Wilder was certainly living up to his reputation for always
thinking he knew best, and not appearing to care who he
offended, providing he got his own way.

For the next eight years the Wilders carried on their work
independently, supported partly by their own presbytery and
partly by gifts from Europeans in India such as Bartle Frere. They
were extremely hard-working, and had 3,300 pupils through
their schools, 500 of whom were girls. Their passionate goal was
to lift up the masses of ordinary people by founding indigenous
schools. These were entirely financed without foreign money.
During the three cool months of the year Royal travelled widely,
preaching in over two thousand villages and leaving a Bible or a
gospel in each one. As with so much pioneer work through the
ages, the results were slow in coming. It was more a time of
ploughing and harrowing the soil, and scattering the seed, rather
than of reaping the harvest. But they managed to gather a small
group of twenty communicants and six children. The humble
beginnings were at last bearing fruit.

Towards the end of this period an Anglo-Catholic British missionary society, the Society for the Propagation of the Gospel, sent a delegate, Bishop Douglas, to inspect the Wilders' schools and church buildings. They then proposed to take them over, at a price fixed by mutual agreement. Royal and Eliza Jane could see no reason for relinquishing their precious work into which they had poured so much love and toil. However, when they left for a year's furlough in 1869–70 the SPG occupied Kolhapur with three missionaries. Bishop Douglas, having failed to buy the Wilders off, had decided the time to move into Kolhapur was during their absence. As news of this reached Royal and Eliza Jane on their return, they protested strongly to the Bishop. They were now working officially under the Presbyterian Board and considered Kolhapur a Presbyterian monopoly. What right had Anglicans to invade their territory? To all protests, the SPG, the Bishop and the Anglican missionaries turned a deaf ear. Although an unhappy correspondence continued for four years, the SPG finally remained in Kolhapur. Looking back on it now, one could say there was room for both missions in such a highly populated area. But it was discourteous to intrude on someone else's work without consultation, and sadly friction continued for many years. Competitive action of this sort always brings dishonour to the name of Christ.

Happily in many countries comity agreements between the various missions have meant that each has respected the other's areas of work. This has reduced the potential for friction considerably. More recently, when entering a previously closed country for the first time, many missionaries have been willing to form one united mission e.g. the United Mission to Nepal, and even later still, the Joint Christian Services in Mongolia. This brings about a spirit of co-operation and gives a united voice when dealing with the local government.

The Wilders were soon encouraged by the Presbyterian Board's sending out reinforcements. Within a few years their new workers were able to start fresh work in neighbouring towns in the Western Ghats. The strategy of their work came from Royal's conviction that 'native churches should have native pastors; that native churches should be self-supporting; that native Christians should be trained to responsibility, and taught to keep on a level with their neighbours' so that they might win them. They advocated the tithing system whereby ten national believers might support a teacher or preacher who was willing to live on their level.

Eliza Jane continued to manage the girls' school and her growing family, and to carry on evangelistic work which often took her to the Maharaja's palace. Their next son, William, returned to America for education, while Robert, their youngest child and my grandfather, was growing up with the loving support of his older sister Grace.

What was Eliza Jane really like? The picture of her that emerges from the records is far more uncertain than that of her husband. The chauvinism typical of that age meant that mission-ary wives were often regarded as mere appendages to their husbands. But she had her own clear sense of call. She was not merely following her husband; she was determined that her presence would help, not hinder the work. In fact, they appear to have been deeply united, dedicated to the same goal of bringing Christ to the Indian people. Working side by side throughout their lives they made a great team.

Eliza Jane was responsible for keeping the home running smoothly, setting Royal free for his tasks, but she exercised her own wide ministry. Unusually for her generation, she had a vision for the needs of Indian women and wanted to develop their potential. From her own experience she knew the significance of womens' education for raising their status. Because she was the first to start a school for girls in the whole State, her work was very influential in opening the door for Indian women later to enter the professions. Eliza Jane's advanced ideas must be seen against the common view of women in those days. Even in the west they were expected to 'know their place'. When the first woman doctor graduated in America about 1850 the *Boston Medical Journal* com-mented: 'It is to be regretted that Miss Blackwell has been induced to depart from the appropriate sphere of her sex and led to aspire to honours and duties which by the order of nature and the common consent of the world devolve upon men.'

Eliza Jane must have been a woman with plenty of character; and as I write, her stern gaze from her last photo almost makes me tremble. Her straight grey hair is parted severely and adorned with a snow-white cap. The high neck and voluminous folds of her dark dress denote a formality I am not used to. The firm set of her mouth speaks of a person who knows her own mind. Yet she is said to have been the gentler one of the two and much easier to relate to. Her granddaughter, Ruth Braisted, comments: 'Her gentle kindliness had won her friends both in the Maharaja's palace and in humble homes. Wherever there was a need she gave of herself unstintingly; but her first loyalty was always to her husband and family.'

Ruth Braisted's account goes on to describe Eliza Jane's and Royal's deep dependence on God and confidence in prayer, especially when funds were running low during the eight years when they worked independently of a missionary society. As I think of Robert, her son and my grandfather, I realize that Eliza Jane will probably have influenced his life just as much as his father did.

Apart from Royal's regular work during those years he developed his prolific writing gifts. He became a regular contributor to the *Times of India* on education policy. The editorials which he wrote greatly influenced the Indian government in establishing a clear education policy. Sir Bartle Frere judged that Royal Wilder 'contributed more to the educational development of India than any other man I know'. As we saw earlier, Royal had dedicated his energies to mastering Marathi. He served faithfully on the committee for translation and revision of the Bible into Marathi, published commentaries on three gospels, and translated many books.

In 1875 the Wilders were forced to return to America because of poor health. But the Christian community in Kolhapur had

now grown to sixty adults, and a promising church and presbytery were well established. Three fine Indian Christians had
been appointed as elders. They had started their training for the
ministry and had already begun to preach. The church continued to grow steadily and by the turn of the century numbered
seven hundred. So the slow and difficult beginning brought very
rewarding progress which was built on solid foundations. It is
interesting to note how the growth of the church coincided
with wider denominational links and more definite church
structures.

1927 saw a Memorial Church to the Wilders being planned,
and this church still stands there today. Typically it was designed
with as much space for Christian education as for worship.

Return to America

Returning to America, the Wilders made their new home in
Princeton, New Jersey, where their health steadily improved.
Royal decided on yet one more literary project: he founded and
edited *The Missionary Review of the World* from 1877–1887, partly
to disseminate his own ideas on the theory of mission. Its
visionary aim was to present the needs and situation of 'all
missions of all denominations throughout all heathendom and
nominal Christendom', while its motto summed up Royal's own
attitude: *Nil desperandum Christo sub duce*, 'Undaunted, under
Christ as leader'. Often he 'struck out at opponents with harsh
condemnations, couched in polite, legalistic language' as one
researcher comments. But through the following years many of
his suggestions were accepted by the Presbyterian Board and even
by the American Board, greatly contributing to their efficiency.
The Missionary Review was one of the best missionary magazines
at the time, becoming a major vehicle for the expression of new
ideas and missionary fervour at the turn of the century. With its
continuation under Dr. A.T. Pierson it left an abiding mark.

As he grew increasingly elderly, Royal never wavered in his missionary vision.

> 'For too long the church has neglected her marching orders . . . her efforts have been faint and few . . . but she is not to wait for some new or miraculous power to accomplish [her task]. . . . I verily believe the church of Christ is able to evangelize the heathen world in one short generation. I believe her resources, under God, are fully adequate to accomplish this task' (*Mission Schools in India* p.420).

He went on to challenge his readers, 'If 100,000 men could be mobilized to crush the Indian Mutiny, why could not an equal number mobilize to serve Christ?'

After twelve years in America this veteran couple still longed to return to India. Royal was now over seventy and had been suffering intense pain for many months. It was more than a year since the doctors had given him only six months to live. Nevertheless with characteristic stubbornness he determined to go back to his beloved Kolhapur to die. Their daughter Grace was now free to go with them and her presence would be a tremendous cheer. But with the sailing date only two weeks away Royal died. Only that very morning he had completed the last page of the last number of the tenth volume of the *Missionary Review*. What driving will-power he must have had to complete this task!

With deep sorrow, and yet undaunted by her loss, his widow resolved to sail nevertheless. She had been called to overseas mission as a child, and all her life she remained true to this vocation. She knew there was still much work to be done in Kolhapur, and she determined not to allow her own grief to hinder the work. Grace went with her mother to cheer and support her. Together mother and daughter saw many years of fruitful service. Grace worked in various roles, acting as principal of a boys' school for a time, and later preparing the study course for 'Bible women' which would be used for many years. While on furlough in 1898 Grace was one of the few women speakers at the Student Volunteer Convention, concerning which more will be said in the next chapter.

As her mother grew older, Grace kept up an incessant pro-gramme of evangelism and poured her energy into this task. With her intimate knowledge of Indian life and culture she recruited five single women to form a 'village settlement'. They hoped to live together as a community and work out from the centre, trusting that before too long they could turn it over to others and start a new settlement elsewhere. Indians were familiar with the idea of a hermit living in an ashram, a communal centre for religious study and practice. Grace's idea fitted Indian community ideals of 'ashram living', and would provide scope for single women in a mission where most of the personnel were married couples. Grace's strategy may remind us of early Celtic monks and their evangelistic methods. But these two strict Presbyterian ladies might have objected to being credited with forming 'monasteries'!

However, the scheme took some time to get off the ground because, although the Board approved, the Mission did not. Oh the heartache of being answerable to several managers!

As the years passed, Eliza Jane grew increasingly frail and her memory declined. Although she became unable to talk very clearly, yet she could express herself powerfully in prayer. After 64 years of missionary service in India Eliza Jane Wilder went to be with the Lord she loved. Sadly her daughter Grace died less than a year later, and was buried together with her mother in the cemetery in their beloved Kohlapur.

What tremendous days Eliza Jane had lived through! She had arrived in India as a young bride in the first half of the previous century. Together with her husband, she had mastered a difficult language, overcome intense hostility, and pioneered women's education in western India. At the same time she ran the home and brought up their children. They had worked as the only Christian missionaries among four million people, enduring a taxing climate and surviving dangerous tropical diseases. Before

Eliza Jane died her Mission had branched out into medical work, building a hospital and later a medical school. Industrial education was also started for the local population.

From humble beginnings, Eliza Jane saw the Christian community in Kohlapur grow into many hundreds of converts with evangelism spreading over a wide area. Soon after she died mass movements to Christ began to take place in the very areas where she and Grace had worked. The number of Christians grew rapidly from approximately 750 to 7,500. How greatly God honoured the sacrifice of a young couple who refused to be daunted by any difficulty if only they could fulfil their Master's will. They were far from perfect. But they left a legacy of total obedience, dedication and determination, coupled with prayerfulness and integrity.

Royal and Eliza Jane had never been rich by worldly standards. I don't know what material possessions they bequeathed to their family. But they did leave their children an intangible legacy, as all parents do − a legacy that could be passed down from generation to generation, independent of what might happen to the economy of the nation or the world. One important part of that legacy was their practice of total obedience to God and, linked to it, a spirit of prayerfulness expressing a concern to know God's will and a sense of dependence on him. Other items in the legacy may appear more 'human' but they were in fact inextricably mingled with the 'godly' elements. For part of the legacy was a commitment, dedication and determination which carried them through the most difficult circumstances. They were in fact not just expressions of individual temperament but grounded in their faith in God. So too was the integrity which marked their lives and which stood in marked contrast to many people's anxiety about their own reputation.

As I have researched this part of the family story I have increasingly come to respect both of my great-grandparents, but not least the qualities shown by Eliza Jane at a time when women's potential was little recognized.

BIBLIOGRAPHY
for Chapters 1 & 2

Braisted, Ruth E., *In This Generation: The Story of Robert P. Wilder* (New York: Friendship Press, 1941)

Schneider, Robert A., 'Royal G. Wilder: New School Missionary in the ABCFM 1846–1871' *American Presbyterian Journal*, 64:2 Summer 1986.

'In Memoriam: Rev. Royal Gould Wilder' *Missionary Review of the World* 11:1 (Jan. 1888)

'Seventy-Fifth Anniversary: Western India Mission of the Presbyterian Church in the United States of America' *Western India Notes*, 10:2 (November 1928).

Beaver, R. Pierce, *The Legacy of Rufus Anderson* (Occasional Bulletin, July 1979).

Shenk, Wilbert R., 'Rufus Anderson and Henry Venn: A Special Relationship?' *International Bulletin of Missionary Research* (October 1981)

Latourette, Kenneth Scott, *A History of Christianity* (London: Eyre and Spottiswoode Ltd, 1954).

Neill, Stephen, *A History of Christian Mission* (Harmondsworth: Pelican, rev. ed. 1986).

Wilder, Royal Gould, *Mission Schools in India of the American Board of Commissioners of Foreign Missions* (New York, 1856).

Chapter 3

A Daunting Target

In 1861 Royal Wilder asserted that 'the Church of Christ is able to evangelize the whole world in one short generation'. Half a century later, 1200 delegates to the first World Missionary Conference, held at Edinburgh in 1910, united to affirm his watchword.

'The evangelization of the world in this generation!' – what an audacious goal! Could it possibly be achieved? Could the whole world be offered the gospel? Indeed, could a group of mere students, none of whom had any influence, realistically contemplate such an achievement? Many well-known Christian leaders scornfully dismissed the idea as a youthful pipe-dream. Others stated categorically that it was completely impossible.

Yet the slogan spread like wild-fire, first through the universities of America, and then across the Atlantic to Britain and continental Europe. It dramatically jolted the lethargic Protestant churches, and thousands of men and women were challenged to volunteer for missionary service. It has been calculated that in the next two decades more than 20,000 missionaries left to serve God overseas as a direct result of this Student Volunteer Movement. Because of its influence a steady stream of recruits continued for a further twenty years. Nothing like it had been seen before in the history of the church.

What inspired this new enthusiasm? In 1886 Dwight L. Moody, the famous evangelist, held the first of his 'College Students' Summer Schools for Bible Study', at Mount Hermon, Massachusetts. Among the delegates was the young Robert Wilder, who had recently graduated from Princeton College.

Three years earlier, the burning missionary vision caught from his parents had led him, together with several other students, to form the Princeton Foreign Missionary Society. Members formally declared: 'We are willing and desirous, God permitting, to become foreign missionaries.' Every Sunday afternoon the Princeton group had met for prayer at the Wilder home, much encouraged by Robert's parents and challenged by a large map of the world which hung on the wall. Royal Wilder often spoke to them of his thirty years' experience in India and challenged them: 'Christ told all his disciples to go. The question is not whether we are called to go, but whether we are called to stay at home!'

With the strict decorum of those days, Robert's sister Grace, with her friends from Mt. Holyoke Seminary, met in an adjoining room praying for God's blessing on this new movement. Brother and sister together longed and prayed that this small group would be the beginning of a new missionary interest among college students to spread across America. As Robert left for the 1886 summer school, Grace confidently asserted, 'I believe our prayers will be answered at Mount Hermon.'

But Moody had not planned to include overseas mission in his programme. 'Our aim is Bible teaching', he stated, 'and the deepening of the spiritual life.' So Robert began quietly to make friends among the many delegates and share the missionary challenge with them. It was thus that one afternoon, when swimming in the river, he met John R. Mott, later to become a world-famous missionary statesman. As they tramped back, Robert challenged him concerning the spiritual needs of the world; and Mott too joined the growing team of young men who signed the Princeton Declaration. Each evening as the sun set, this group met for prayer and shared their missionary concerns.

After two conference weeks of memorable fellowship and Bible teaching Robert went to Moody and asked if ten of his friends might be allowed to speak briefly on overseas mission at one of the evening meetings. Moody agreed, allowing each one just three minutes to present the needs of a different area of the world. The reporter for the *Springfield Republican* described the first speaker as:

> '. . . a young man born in India and bred for the eastern mission field, whose fire and zeal gleamed underneath a quiet exterior as he marshalled his facts."

This young man was Robert Wilder, who spoke for India. Nine others followed him, representing Persia (Iran), Siam (Thailand), Japan, Armenia, the Sioux Indians and others. John Mott, writing later about 'The Meeting of the Ten Nations', as it has come to be called, believed that it might 'occupy as significant a place in the history of the Christian Church as the Williams Haystack Meeting'.

During the days that followed many students, with quiet sober determination, took the step of making Christ not only Saviour but complete Lord of their lives. The numbers who felt led to sign the Declaration swelled to seventy-six. Some days later Robert asked D.L. Moody if Dr. A.T. Pierson, his father's great friend, could speak at one of the evening meetings. The theme Pierson chose was: 'The evangelization of the world in this generation'. This became Robert's watchword for the newly emerging movement, echoing the vision of his father and my great-grandfather.

Before leaving for the conference, Robert and Grace had prayed together for a hundred new missionaries. Then on the last night when ninety-nine volunteers were praying together long after the others had gone to bed, one more man joined them. So they praised God that their target of a hundred had been reached.

With the launching of the Student Volunteer Movement it was decided that Robert Wilder together with some friends should tour the universities for a year to carry the challenge right across America. What sort of person was Robert Wilder? And how had God brought him to this point?

Childhood Experiences

Robert had spent his first twelve years in India, becoming fully steeped in the local life and culture. As there were no separate schools for missionaries' children in those days, he attended his father's schools along with the local children. He often went visiting with his mother and older sister, so felt as much at home with the poorest as with the richest in the land. He learnt to ride with one of the princes and much enjoyed racing over the countryside. But he was a sensitive child who loved music and would often curl up in a corner listening as others played their precious piano, an almost unheard-of luxury in those remote parts.

One day when Grace was at the keys, unknown to her a large cobra coiled itself around the pedals as she played. She noticed it only as she walked away, and at once called out for her father. He shouted to his Indian servant to help; but the old man refused to move a muscle. After Royal himself had rapidly killed the snake, he demanded to know why the man refused to help him. 'How do I know?' he replied. 'Maybe my grandfather was in that snake.'

As he watched, the young Robert received an indelible impression of how deep-seated was the Indian belief in reincarnation. He knew he must come back to India as a missionary when he grew up. Although only ten years old, he began reading the New Testament every day to this servant, urging him to believe in Christ.

But when two years later the family settled back in America, Robert found it difficult to fit in. He missed his Indian friends and the familiar scenery of his childhood. American life felt very artificial and his sensitivity made him shy. Having such an articulate and determined father it is perhaps not surprising that Robert felt unsure of himself. Growing up in the shadow of such a powerful figure, and now facing the huge change of culture, his self-confidence was deeply undermined. Maybe he found his refuge in books and academic achievement; we know that his mother often had to warn him against burying himself in books. Eliza Jane feared for him as he was not physically strong. 'Rest your soul on Jesus, and be content to do according to your strength', she advised.

However he still felt his sense of responsibility for overseas mission very keenly, and at high school tried to interest his friends. 'But every time I spoke in public', he wrote later, 'it seemed to be a failure, owing to my shyness. So one day I told my sister that the missionary call could not be obeyed because public speaking was impossible. She took me in hand with a faith and courage which inspired me. "With Christ nothing is impossible," she said.' With her encouragement Robert persevered and began to work hard at mastering his nervousness in public speaking. Later he was rewarded by winning the school prize for oratory.

In his last years at high school the shyness and nervousness which had made him so tongue-tied were at last being conquered. He was learning to use the twin tools of tackling a problem head-on with hard work while at the same time trusting God for his help. Where his father's strong personality had cramped his spirit, Robert was now discovering that he need not be a prisoner to his upbringing. While appreciating greatly the rich heritage of missionary vision his parents had given him, Robert was developing his own personality. Throwing himself fully into the life all around him, he was able to overcome the earlier handicap of the huge cultural readjustment he had had to make on leaving India.

Touring for SVM

The initial euphoria which came with launching SVM was immediately challenged by difficulties. Three other men had agreed to accompany Robert on their tour of the colleges. One

by one they all dropped out, including John Mott. The reasons
were beyond their control but Robert was left with a huge
responsibility. Would the whole movement collapse before it had
ever really got off the ground?

A further blow came as Royal Wilder was taken ill and the
doctors gave him only six months to live. Robert's older brother
and his wife wrote scathingly against his plans: 'To join this "band
of Missionary Troubadours" is of doubtful utility and propriety.'
But once again Grace strengthened his resolve. 'Nothing worth-
while is ever accomplished without surmounting great obstacles,'
she assured him.

For two days Robert's sick father said nothing. Then one day
he called him to his study. 'Son, let the dead bury their dead. Go
thou and preach the kingdom,' Royal said. The old warrior was
still ready for sacrifice to the very end. Later he took great
comfort from the knowledge that his poor health had not
obstructed God's work.

Another son of missionaries, John Forman, was willing to
travel with Robert and together they visited forty-four colleges.
Robert's health, which was never robust, gave way early on. But
after a time of earnest prayer they felt they should press on,
because 'the success of the movement was worth the price of
risking one person's breakdown'. Although at times so weak he
could hardly stand while speaking, he persevered and ended the
very demanding year in better health than when he began.
Robert had certainly inherited some of his parents' determination. For a while Forman was called away to care for his sick
brother. By the close of the eight month tour they could report
162 colleges visited. John Mott, describing these early days of
SVM, says, 'Their straightforward, forcible, scriptural presentation came with convincing power to the minds and hearts of
students wherever they went. Not an institution was visited in
which they did not quicken the missionary interest.'

Over two thousand volunteers signed their declaration. Grace,
who constantly supported her brother in prayer, wrote, 'I almost

envy you young men when I think of the host of girls which might be enlisted also.' But they were enlisting girls as well, and 550 young women were among that first two thousand. Many future well-known missionaries dated their missionary call to this period, including Samuel Zwemer, the great apostle to Muslims, and Robert Speer, chairman of the Presbyterian Mission Board for many years.

The Holy Spirit and Prayer

Robert and John Forman were very conscious of their weakness and mistakes. They attributed the astounding results to the work of the Holy Spirit. Four years earlier Robert had heard Dr A. J. Gordon of Boston preach powerfully on the Holy Spirit. Deeply impressed by what he had heard, Robert went to question him afterwards. 'Must I also wait twenty years before I can get this same power in my life?' Gordon replied, 'God is ready to give you the power of the Holy Spirit as soon as you are ready to surrender fully to him.' Robert linked this answer to Acts 5:32: '. . . the Holy Spirit whom God gives to those who obey him'. Robert resolved, as far as he was able, to live a life of holiness and obedience.

The Holy Spirit's working and the power of prayer formed the double spring-board that launched the movement. Someone closely involved commented, 'There was much, very much prayer underlying all this Movement, and there was an utter casting of ourselves on God, and willingness to follow the Spirit's leading. This had much to do with the depth of the Movement.'

It was above all from his mother that Robert had learned the importance of prayer. He remembered how all through their years in India she had set apart a day a month for prayer and fasting. Each Sunday evening after the many services were ended she took Robert and Grace into the west room of the Mission bungalow and they would pray together for their older brothers in America. It was there, with his mother's encouragement, that he had learned to pray aloud.

After the exhilaration of this first tour John Forman sailed for India where he gave thirty years of devoted service with the Presbyterian Board. He was in such a hurry to leave that he did not complete his studies; but although Robert was already familiar with India, he knew it was important to be as fully prepared as possible. For his future work among the educated classes of India Robert felt the need of theological training. He had no desire to be ordained, as he felt it might act as a barrier between him and the students. A degree in theology, however, would deepen his understanding of Scripture and enable him to hold his own in philosophical discussions. With a wisdom born of years of experience, his father endorsed his decision: 'Time spent in sharpening tools is not time wasted.'

So in the autumn of 1887 Robert entered Union Theological Seminary, New York, and his parents sold their home in Princeton, preparing to return to India. But, as we have seen, Royal Wilder died before he could set off. He had placed his journal, *The Missionary Review of the World*, in the capable hands of his friend, A.T. Pierson. Eliza Jane and Grace bravely clung to their original plan and sailed two weeks later.

SVM continues to develop

Although there was now no one travelling the colleges on behalf of SVM, the number of volunteers continued to grow. In spite of the demands of his theological studies, Robert remained the virtual leader, arranging meetings, speaking himself, corresponding with churches and mission boards and advising volunteers. A fellow student, William Hannum, also later to serve in India, helped with the filing and kept the records of names and addresses of the volunteers. Having nowhere else to store them, the cards were kept under his bed! Later when the Movement was formally organized, William became its first secretary. 'I know you are doing the work of three ordinary fellows,' was the comment John Mott made to Robert about his heavy programme that year. Like his father, Robert was never afraid of hard work.

So in July the following year it was decided that SVM must appoint a full-time worker. John Mott, just graduated from Cornell University, was the unanimous choice for this new executive leader. Already his marked ability and keen insight had given him leadership roles in his own college and in the Student Young Men's Christian Association. These qualities, combined with an evangelistic compassion and missionary enthusiasm, made him the obvious choice for the first chairman. For over thirty years he led the SVM very ably and presided at the first nine quadrennial conventions. These later led into the highly influential Urbana conferences which today challenge many thousands of students to face the needs of the world.

While shouldering his new responsibilities, John Mott urged Robert Wilder to give a second year to travelling across the continent to develop and extend the SVM. This would mean interrupting his theological studies and delay his preparation for going to India; so Robert prayed much about it, as he did about every decision of his life. Finally he felt this was indeed God's call to him and threw all his energies into another extensive tour.

Problems of Finance

With the large number of volunteer missionaries came a comparable need for finance to support them. The missionary societies could not raise the additional money to cope with such a flood, so the SVM executive committee thrashed out a new strategy. The responsibility for finance should be shouldered by their sending church or by a group of college students. John Mott and Robert Wilder set out to tour the country and challenge each college or church to take responsibility for the salary of one missionary or couple. This was a completely new venture. So it was with some trepidation that they began asking for pledged money. However, soon forty colleges and as many churches gladly agreed with the plan. But some people were critical, 'People ought to give money not out of interest in particular objects, but out of love for Christ.' How true! Sadly the human heart often needs other forms of motivation before it will be stirred to action.

The volunteers themselves often spoke at meetings. One wrote to Robert, 'I spoke 22 times in 22 days! Six or seven churches at least have taken 'the Plan' (i.e. agreed to support a missionary)'. This man suffered from the heavy handicap of a bad stammer, but found he never stammered when speaking on overseas mission! Many of them used the highwayman's challenge: 'Your money or your life!', saying 'We have given our lives. Won't you give the money to support us?'

Samuel Zwemer's report conveys the atmosphere of those days. He was appealing for money on behalf of his colleague, James Cantine, and James in turn was raising funds for him:

> 'Travelled about 4,000 miles and visited nearly every church of our denomination west of Ohio. Much encouragement, some discouragement. Lethargy of the pastors is the great drawback . . . After a desperate struggle have paid all my bills, and now stand on the same basis as Adam when he commenced business – no capital, but plenty of pluck.' [We presume however that he was more fully clothed!]

This new challenge to give to the work of mission had an interesting result. Ever since this time, missionary giving in America has largely been directed towards the support of an individual, not towards the general expenses of a Society as was customary in Britain. This means the giving is very personal and flexible. Because each individual raises their own support, the missionary society can grow in size almost without limit as may be seen today in the large membership of some outstanding missions which were founded by Americans. A weakness may be that supporters may lose interest when their own particular missionary returns home. In contrast, the earlier method in Britain encouraged people to take a wide and long-term interest in the whole work of a particular mission. This will not wane if their own missionary returns, and the interest will embrace a far wider area than just the work of their own missionary. With more recent financial difficulties, many British societies have moved closer to the American model. But strengths and weaknesses can be seen in both approaches.

Spiritual Blessing

A new movement of spiritual life seemed to spring from the SVM meetings. At Knoxville, Tennessee, Robert and John spoke at a conference and thirty students decided to accept Christ as Saviour and Lord. When delegates from that conference went back to their colleges, they led from twelve to fifty other students in each college to faith in Christ.

There were many other similar testimonies. For instance, a missionary about to sail wrote to Robert, 'Your action last spring has put two more missionaries in the field. But this is a very small part of it all. The effect of the whole proceeding on the United Presbyterian Church cannot be measured. Quite a revival is in process among us which is to be traced very largely to last spring.' So once more it became clear that where concern for overseas mission is stirred up this often leads to revival in the local church. The influence of this small group of dedicated volunteers was spreading like ripples in a pool, reaching far more people than they would ever have imagined.

In his speaking Robert repeatedly emphasized the biblical basis for mission, reminding his hearers that 'the most important theme in the Bible is missionary work'. He explained how the golden thread running right through its pages is God's love for a rebellious world. God prepared for, and then sent, his Son to redeem us all. The natural response of the disciples to the climactic events of Christ's death, resurrection and ascension was an explosion in missionary concern which is portrayed so clearly in the book of Acts. Before many decades had passed, the gospel had spread from Jerusalem right across to Rome, the strategic centre of the Empire.

Robert illustrated his talks with large maps and elaborate charts which dramatically pointed out the needs of the large, unevangelized territories of the world. The chart he most often used consisted of: 856 black squares representing 856 million 'heathen', 170 green squares representing 170 million Muslims, and in the centre 2 white squares representing the Protestant Christians in non-Christian lands. Its impact was very striking.

He emphasized how responding to the missionary challenge could bring blessing to the home church. Pungently he claimed that:

> 'As metaphysics may be called the pure mathematics of theology, so missions are its practical application. They are destined to play an important part in correcting the vagaries of theologians [sic!], as practical engineering has done in the domain of theoretical mechanics.'

A hundred years later Professor Andrew Walls of Aberdeen University made a similar point, writing in the *International Bulletin of Missionary Research* (15 October 1991).

> 'Contemporary theology needs renewal by mission studies . . . It needs to grapple with the history, thought and life of the churches of the non-Western world and of the missionary movement that was their catalyst, the understanding of Christian history and of the nature of Christian faith which studies of these topics bring. . . . Western theology, however, resembles Singapore in 1942: though well equipped with heavy weaponry, most of it points in the wrong direction.'

The rising tide of challenge to mission had its effect in the theological seminaries. The theory of mission and the biblical basis for mission began to be studied and taught. John Mott, commenting later on the far-reaching legacy of SVM, wrote: 'It has planted missionary libraries or missionary sections in libraries already existing, in over 400 colleges and theological seminaries' and, he continued, it 'did more than any other agency to usher in the modern mission study movement'.

In consequence the U.S.A. has subsequently led the world in teaching the practice of mission and also in missionary research, although their missiology is often pragmatic and sociological. Even in the U.S.A. a false dichotomy is often still seen between missiology and biblical theological studies. Surely missiology lies at the heart of all theology, and runs like a scarlet thread throughout the Bible! What about the United Kingdom? Sadly in Britain, although God's heart for mission lies at the centre of biblical revelation, missiology remains a cinderella subject in most seminaries and Bible colleges.

Underlining the far-reaching effects of the SVM on American churches, Mott continued:

> 'The influence of the movement on the religious life of the colleges . . . of North America has been both wide and profound. It is not too much to say that within this past generation the outlook of a multitude of Christian students has been changed from the provincial to the cosmopolitan. . . . Limited ideas have fast given way to enlarged conceptions of the grandeur . . . of this greatest work which confronts the church of God.'

How wonderfully God had answered the prayer of a brother and sister who dared to ask great things for his kingdom! The legacy which Royal and Eliza Jane passed on was being multiplied into blessing to thousands of people.

The remarkable thing about a family legacy of this kind is the way it is able to develop and multiply. We have already paused to recognize that Grace's 'achievement' may seem small by comparison with that of other family members. But her input into Robert's life and thus into his 'achievement' was of great importance. And it derived from the same family legacy which in Robert's life took a form which his parents could scarcely have foreseen. For Robert was not only a 'missionary'. He was an inspirer of many others. Through his ministry thousands of missionaries went to tell others of Christ.

The Missionary Volunteers were quick to recognize the value of literature and publicity for extending their impact; they produced a series of pamphlets, including *Shall I go?* by Grace Wilder and *The Bible and Mission* by Robert Wilder. Speakers were urged to make these widely available. In addition, *The Missionary Review* was offered at a generous price to any Volunteer thanks to a special arrangement with its editor, A.T. Pierson. Robert also ordered from Britain a thousand copies of *The Evangelization of the World – A Missionary Band* by Benjamin Broomhall of the CIM. This sold very well and aroused deep interest as it gave the story of the Cambridge Seven. These seven Cambridge undergraduates, privileged, wealthy and highly educated, had offered themselves for missionary service following Moody's mission to the University in 1887. The many books and pamphlets strongly increased the impact of the SVM speakers. Robert had learned from the prolific writings of his father how literature can influence people.

With SVM now under the capable leadership of John Mott and his own theological studies completed, Robert Wilder made plans for sailing to India at last. The Presbyterian Board commissioned him to work among students in India 'on an undenominational basis'. Significantly, five other leading mission boards of North America who had been impressed by his achievements joined in commissioning him. Each wrote letters commending him to the representatives of their respective churches. This was a unique event, and highlights another spin-off from the SVM. Ruth Rouse in *A History of the Ecumenical Movement* comments:

'No voluntary movement has been more powerful in drawing
the churches together than the SVM. . . . It had a peculiar power
to knit together its members in the close fellowship of their
common and mighty adventure.'

In those days when denominational lines were drawn very rigidly
SVM was far ahead of its time. This was expressed by one of the
Cambridge Seven who became the first secretary for the British
SVM:

'SVM aims at banding together all students whose hearts are
stirred up by the Holy Spirit to obey our Master's parting
command . . . Feeling the pulse of Christian students where I
have visited, I have found that they seem just ripe for such a
movement, welding into one union our students – Episcopalian,
Presbyterian, Wesleyan, Baptist and Methodist alike – united into
a brotherhood hitherto thought to be impossible.'

Robert, who never felt himself tied by denominations, must have
rejoiced at what was happening.

Visit to Britain

In response to numerous requests from British delegates to the
SVM conferences, Robert decided to break his journey to India
with a stop-over in Britain. Now 27 years old, he crossed the
Atlantic in June 1891. On board ship he had an interesting
conversation with the Rev. Ellinwood, Secretary of the Presbyterian Board. Referring to Christian work in the Far East
Ellinwood commented: 'The whole world is coming rapidly
under the influence of European languages and literature, the
English holding a larger place than any other. In medicine, for
example, it would be far easier to give young men a knowledge
of English than to undertake the translation of a large number of
medical books into Arabic, Chinese, or Hindi.' To Robert, who
must have been aware of his Father's sharp disagreement with

the ABCFM over the use of English, this must have come as
music to the ears.

On landing Robert spent three days in prayer and waiting on
God, wondering how best to introduce SVM to the universities
of Britain. Some had suggested he enrol as a student at a university
like Oxford and gradually build up a force of volunteers; others
that he should try to set up a tour as he had done back home.
Worshipping in the majestic Canterbury Cathedral on the Sunday afternoon he heard a helpful sermon on 'Courage'. Significantly, he noted in his journal the preacher's challenge, 'To
shrink from fear of ridicule is more cowardly than to run away
in battle.' This indicates something of Robert's struggles at the
time. With his limited strength because of his health, and feeling
alone among strangers, this sermon encouraged Robert as he
faced an unknown future. 'Christ was very near today,' he wrote
in his journal, 'I gave myself to him entirely and decided to take
one step at a time, trusting solely in him and not leaning to my
own understanding.'

God had his loving plans for both Robert and the new
movement. There would be no need to wait for the university
year to begin in October. Proceeding to London, Robert made
use of his many letters of introduction (including fourteen from
D.L. Moody) to obtain interviews with leading Christians. The
outcome was an invitation to the Keswick Convention later that
very month to tell his remarkable story.

He was invited to stay with Mrs. MacInnes, wife of an MP
and mother of the secretary of the Cambridge Inter-Collegiate
Christian Union. Her daughter described Robert's arrival: 'Er-
skine Lodge, Keswick, was tightly packed with visitors (and) the
house party were all very spontaneous and unconventional. "Do
remember to behave when our American guest comes – he
probably is very old with a long white beard," we said. . . . (Then)
there skipped to the entrance a very alert-much-all-there young
man, carrying a back-pack, and asking almost at once, "Is there

a stenographer round the corner?" ' A great friendship grew out of this stay; and throughout the years Robert was a welcome visitor at their homes in Cumbria and in London.

Robert begged for more than the official five minutes at the missionary meeting: 'I can never say all that I want to tell in those few moments.' In the thirteen that he was grudgingly allowed he gave, in the words of Eugene Stock, editor of the CMS magazine, 'a brief but thrilling account of the Student Volunteer Movement in America.' People were 'struck by the deep earnestness and sanity' of the presentation. As he finished speaking, 'insistent calls came from all over the tent, "Go on! Go on!" ' At the close of the meeting they flocked to talk with him and invite him to their universities.

Robert was thrilled with these opportunities. He realized God was showing him clearly the way forward. But yet again poor health hindered him. Not physically strong, he still found it almost impossible to say 'no' to any opportunity to extend God's kingdom. This was a problem that dogged him all through his life. Perhaps the work ethic of his parents goaded him unnecessarily. Yet because of his drive he achieved much. His limited strength also created a lovely humility and a deep dependence on God.

Norwegian Interlude

The doctors now insisted on an extended period of rest and recuperation. But even weakness can be turned into blessing by our gracious God. Together with a friend from America Robert set out on a walking tour of Norway, a land which had fascinated him from childhood. On the ship going over, his gently outgoing manner led to a friendship with a young Norwegian, who invited the two Americans to visit his home in Gjøvik on lovely Lake Mjøsa. When they arrived after several weeks walking, their friend was not at home. So his mother, who spoke no English, hurried next door for help.

Helene Valborg Olssøn, who arrived to be their interpreter, was helping her widowed mother run a small guest house. It later developed into the famous Victoria Hotel which boasted renowned rose gardens and lovely lakes crossed by picturesque bridges. When Robert met Helene he fell in love with her on the spot. The two Americans lingered in Gjøvik for eight days, enjoying her company. Robert's friend described her as 'a brunette with very brown eyes and lovely Nordic complexion – very fair to look upon'. Robert wrote to his brother about this Norwegian girl who had so completely captivated his heart, 'She has the dignity and depth – the strength and beauty – of a Viking's daughter. There are in her a grace and refinement – a love of truth and candour which win friends – while the Norwegian reserve and strength of character are well marked.' He was obviously head–over–heels!

Before the eight days were over they had agreed to correspond, and before December was out, a bunch of roses announced that he was on her doorstep again. The next day when a walk in the country brought the coveted 'yes' Robert's joy was complete. He wrote: 'For long I had rested on the promise "He shall choose our inheritance for us", and it was a very deep joy to enter into that inheritance.'

Lovely days were spent together among the green pines and white snow of a Norwegian Christmas, while Robert became acquainted with her family. How hard it was going to be for her widowed mother, Leonora Rebekka, to have her darling Helene whisked away to distant India! It says much for Leonora's commitment to her Lord that she encouraged them to move forward.

Robert wanted to give Helene the best gift he could, so he promised after the wedding in the summer to learn to speak Norwegian.

An Inter-collegiate Movement

In time his strength returned, and Robert was back in Britain in January. A full programme awaited him – Edinburgh, Glasgow, Aberdeen, Cambridge, Oxford and London. Everywhere there was an enthusiastic response from the students as men and women began volunteering for overseas mission. The time seemed ripe to form a British Student Volunteer Movement. But the obstacles were many. The students felt 'American ways' might not catch on in Britain; and anyway it would be too difficult to arrange an inter-collegiate society. This had never been done previously. Before telephones were common, let alone faxes and e-mail, communication even within one country was not easy. Each university had its own strong character. But, like his father before him, Robert was not easily overcome by difficulties.

J.H. Maclean, a Scottish student who later became a missionary to India, recalled:

> 'The charm of Wilder's manner and his genial humour won the attention of the students, and his seriousness and spiritual earnestness made a deep impression. The enthusiasm aroused was wonderful. To this day I remember the glow of it, and the willingness of the early volunteers to undertake whatever toil was involved in their new propaganda. The women were as keen as the men.'

So in April 1892, after much prayer and discussion between groups of students from Cambridge, London, Oxford, the Scottish universities and Ireland, it was decided to form the Student Volunteer Missionary Union of Great Britain and Ireland. The same Declaration was to be undertaken by each member: 'We are willing and desirous, God permitting, to become foreign missionaries.' Cambridge appeared to be the most responsive of the universities. By the end of one term sixty-eight men had signed, including many medical students.

The momentum was such that the following year it was felt that a broader union was needed: an inter-collegiate union which not only challenged for overseas mission but also aimed to bring British students to Christ and build them up in their faith. A conference was held in Keswick the following year to plan for this. Out of this came the British Colleges Christian Union, which was later called the Student Christian Movement. It was set up with three departments, of which the SVMU was one, with its own executive and budget. Donald Fraser, who with 'zeal, courage and vision' became its first leader, had received his call to mission on the day when Robert spoke so movingly at Keswick.

This was an historic development. The establishment of SCM through the influence of Robert Wilder led in future years to the development of many interdenominational student minis-tries. The Inter-Varsity Fellowship (now the Universities and Colleges Christian Fellowship) separated from the SCM in 1920, feeling the latter had grown too politically and socially minded and too theologically liberal. The example of the IVF/UCCF gave rise to the founding of such groups as the Navigators and Campus Crusade for Christ. All these have become international movements with branches in the universities of many countries.

So the legacy of Robert Wilder has reached down through the years to the whole student world, and played a vital part in the development of the church of God. Many who were challenged to give up everything for God while at university became Christian leaders of great influence.

One of the most powerful metaphors Jesus used to describe the nature of the Kingdom of God was when he compared it to yeast. In Robert Wilder's student work we see another aspect of the Christian family legacy. Its influence spreads and goes on working. For the Student Volunteer Movement achieved far more than 'merely' prompting several thousand young people to volunteer for missionary service at the turn of the century. Christian work among students world-wide is a powerful evangelistic force. And thousands of students continue to volunteer for service overseas; more than 10,000 are challenged to meet every three years at the Urbana (Illinois) missionary student conference. A truly Christian family legacy spreads wider and wider.

Towards the close of summer 1891 Robert had the opportunity to meet Christian leaders in Norway and Denmark, and so seeds were sown for the establishing of SVM in Scandinavia.

In this way the prayers of a brother and sister and a small group of students at Princeton, USA were being answered in ways they never dreamed of. Truly God is 'able to do immeasurably more than all we ask or imagine' (Eph.3:20). A life totally given to holiness and dedication to God's will alone can affect the history of countless other people.

Evangelizing the World

At a conference in Sweden in 1895 the World Student Christian Federation was formed. After a whole night of prayer it was decided to accept as the official watchword Robert's original slogan, 'The evangelization of the world in this generation'. They fully believed that, by God's grace, the whole Christian church could be mobilized to fulfil the responsibility outlined in Christ's final command. If hundreds and thousands of men and women volunteered for this task, and supporters at home supplied the necessary prayer backing and finance, there was no reason why the generation alive at that time should not have the chance to hear of the Saviour who died for them. Of course they realized it would be a much longer and more complicated task to disciple the new believers and build them into missionary-minded churches who would then reach out to others. But that could come in the wake of the primary goal of giving everyone the chance to hear.

Their expectation was not unreasonable. In many ways the time for this advance was ripe. It was before two major world wars would shatter the confidence of Christians. Liberal criticism undermining the authority of Scripture had not yet gripped the theological colleges. Steam power was making travel easier and saving weeks of tedious ocean voyaging. Railways were being laid across continents, so the messengers of the gospel could sometimes travel in comparative comfort and speed. Looking back, it is to be regretted that there was not an even greater response by the Christian church at that strategic time when Islam had not yet discovered the power and confidence which came in the wake of oil money, and Buddhism and Hinduism were increasingly seen to be unable to meet spiritual needs. The resurgence of these other faiths was still in the future. But gratitude remains for what God did accomplish through his servants at that time.

Chapter 4

To All the World

For Robert, arrival in India felt like a home-coming, but for Helene everything must have appeared strange. What a help her husband will have been to her, to explain new customs and interpret baffling situations. They were given a wonderful welcome in Kohlapur. Robert was thrilled to see the church had greatly expanded in the eight years since his parents had worked there. And the legacy of his Indian childhood meant he could preach directly in Marathi without an interpreter and deeply understand the hearts of the local people.

But it was work among the more educated to which the young couple felt called. So they responded to an invitation to work with the YMCA in Calcutta for three months and see what that led on to. Education at all levels was now widely accepted as a tool for missionary work, and Calcutta held the reputation of being the largest and most strategic student centre in India. Lecturing in a variety of colleges, Robert invited students to visit him and discuss the Christian faith. But for ten days nobody came. 'Should I have been less evangelistic in my presentation?' he wondered. 'Should I have offered them some other intellectual bait?'

But at last one man came to visit, and returned again and again with questions, hungry for spiritual truth. Others followed, until sometimes he held fifteen or sixteen private talks a day. They came not only from Christian colleges but from Hindu ones as well. Further lectures drew more visitors, some just to argue, others to listen or read the gospels. Where the discussions were in English, and when Helene had the time, she would join in.

Her main task at the moment was language study, but always she was praying in the background.

Brahmin opposition

It was one thing for Hindus to agree in their heart that Christ was the only way to God, but quite another for them to be baptised. Two brahmin men who at last took this step were forcibly removed from the city by their relatives. Only one was ever allowed to visit them again, and that under guard – a chance to 'preach to the jailers as well as the prisoner', Robert recorded.

The three months in Calcutta grew to eighteen, by which time Robert felt that the evangelistic work there was well established. In July 1895 Robert and Helene moved to Poona (now Pune), the centre of orthodox Brahminism in western India, and another strategic student centre. Knowing the country so well and with his burning passion to bring people to know his Lord and Saviour, Robert decided on a high-profile approach to gain as much publicity as possible.

He hired a big, ramshackle theatre situated in a crowded, noisy street in the heart of the city. It was dark and dirty, with great holes in the roof which let in the rain and air but here it would be easy to gather an audience. Starting his lectures with apposite quotations from Indian literature, Robert went on to explain the gospel clearly. He finished by inviting his listeners to come for further discussion to a hall which they were planning to rent as a more permanent centre. These lectures caused a great stir. On the opening day twenty men turned up at the hall and a Bible class on John's Gospel was soon started. Copies of the New Testament were given as prizes to those who came every night for two weeks.

But as had previously happened with Royal, the brahmin leaders began to get agitated at the growing interest. They would shout and argue in the meetings; and soon several students who had shown interest disappeared, forbidden to attend any more.

The climax came when Govind Bhide, a brahmin who had been a believer for two years, had the courage to be baptised and tore off his brahmin sacred thread. As he gave his testimony the next evening it was like 'throwing a lighted match into a powder magazine'. He was kicked and punched and it was all the missionaries could do to get him safely away.

The next evening the storm burst in even greater fury. Someone in the audience cried out in honour of the god Ganpati, and the angry crowd on the street tried to tear up the Bibles. Robert attempted to quieten the mob. But missiles started flying, and there was nothing for it but to beat a hasty retreat.

Yet they were back the next night – only to be met with a hail of stones. 'Stickability' was certainly something Robert had inherited from his parents. And so it went on, with some students hungry for the truth and others determined to break up the meetings. Once, when their words had been drowned out by men thumping with their umbrellas on the floor, they had to retreat through the stage door. The small group of Indian Christians and missionaries stood together in the dark, feeling utterly discouraged. But Robert quietly affirmed, 'This is not failure!' He had learnt from his father never to give up. God will always make a way through the storm.

Govind Bhide was the first Pune brahmin to be baptised in eighteen years, and the owner of the hall dared not stand against the tremendous opposition which erupted. However, after much prayer a new hall was found and the work continued. 'Prayer upset every device of our adversaries,' Robert commented. And when his baby daughter Elizabeth was baptised, two more brahmins followed shortly. Helene often wondered if her husband would return safely from his meetings. Happily her common sense and natural optimism balanced Robert's sensitive nature, and he relied much on her prayer support. Every morning they would start by reading a chapter of the Bible together. Throughout the forty years of their marriage they continued this practice of reading consecutively through the Bible.

After five years in India the Wilders left for furlough in North
America, spending their time mainly with their first concern, the
Student Volunteer Movement. They were asked to help bring
the theological students into the newly formed World Student
Christian Federation and deepen their interest in foreign missions. These were both tasks after their own hearts. They would
often stress unity across denominations, as well as the challenge
to world mission.

Apparently their responding to this request from John Mott
created some strain between them and the Presbyterian Board of
Foreign Missions. The Board hesitatingly granted them leave.
Later, however, the Wilders quietly resigned so as to be free for
wider ministry. In contrast to his father, Robert was pre-eminently
a peacemaker and aimed at maintaining good relationships with
everyone.

During this furlough Robert and Helene were able to visit
Europe and encourage the SVM groups in Britain and Scandinavia. They also had the joy of attending the first SVM conference
in Germany. The tide of mission concern continued to swell. But
at the same time Robert sensed two great weaknesses in the
theological colleges – a lack of devotional, biblical teaching and a
great ignorance concerning world-wide mission. Even today some
might feel these inadequacies have not yet been rectified.

Back in India, Robert and Helene threw themselves into work
among students once more. Robert was responsible for YMCA
work throughout northern and western India. This involved him
in ceaseless travel, often for weeks at a time. Helene was then
left to cope with their growing family. In this situation it was her
bright, even temperament and confident faith in her heavenly
Father's care which carried her through. Robert gave himself
unstintingly to his work, often continuing far beyond the limits
of his physical strength. His diary speaks again and again of
tiredness, headaches and sleepless nights. But 'God helped me'
was a frequent comment. 'Before speaking I felt near collapsing.
As soon as I was on my feet, weariness and fear left. So God

answers prayer.' Like his father before him, he showed dogged determination to fulfil what he saw as the will of God, whatever the cost.

In spite of being such an acceptable public speaker, Robert preferred talking with individuals. He also felt this was more appropriate culturally. He wrote: 'The longer one works in the colleges, the clearer becomes the conviction that seeing men one by one pays better than meetings. Though meetings are necessary to prepare the way.' In this way, with his love and winsomeness, he could probe more deeply into each person's needs, and suit his counsel to their situation.

Was it his father's strong personality which had created in him a dislike of the limelight? He frequently mistrusted his own ability, and self-criticism made him keenly aware of his own shortcomings. Yet as he threw himself on the grace of God this low self-esteem became an asset rather than a hindrance, as it stamped him with a beautiful gentleness and humility.

Wherever he travelled he spoke to people about Christ – to a Scottish engineer he met on a train, to British soldiers in their barracks, to an Indian tailor who called on Sunday for his pay. He especially welcomed the opportunity when a brahmin travelling alone joined him in his railway compartment on a long journey.

A vision of the Lord

His diary at this time records a unique event when he had a vivid experience of Christ. Early one morning he was sitting at his desk with a pile of unanswered letters and an unfinished article staring at him. He had a sermon to prepare for that evening, but four villagers were waiting outside to see him, and the sound of a sharp quarrel breaking out reached his ears.

> Weary in body, distracted in mind, I knew not which way to turn. . . . Just in the moment of despair there was a knock at the

door and a voice said, 'It is the time for communion.' I replied, 'This morning must be an exception. There are three days' work to be done before sunset . . .' Just then the door shut and the speaker vanished. Something prompted me to see who it was . . . As I reached the door I found the retreating form was that of the Lord. I laid hold of him and brought him back. And when the door was locked and we were alone, he placed the pierced hand on my brow and gently soothing out the furrows he said, 'Thou art troubled and cumbered about much serving, but one thing is needful.' Words cannot describe the tender rebuke and exhortation which flowed from his lips. Oh how my heart burned as he opened to me the Scriptures and how the load was lifted as he took it upon his own shoulders.

Then I went out to the veranda, but without the preparation I had planned . . . but as I spoke their opposition ceased, their hearts were melted. . . . The Lord stood next to me, he did the talking, I was only the mouthpiece . . . Then I went to the quarrelling Christians, but with tight hold of the Master's hand. I would not let him go. And an interview which would have been one of the most difficult did not frighten me because he was present. . . . [In speaking to one of the 'quarreling Christians'] my surprise was almost as great as that of the women who found the stone rolled away at the Sepulchre. The angel of the Lord had been there before me. . . . He began to weep like a child. He said it was the look of love in my face. But I know it was the Lord standing by me. He did not see him, but he saw the reflected light from my face.

When I came back to my study . . . his voice said, 'I was the one who told you to write that article. Would you be pleased if your servants made their purchases at the bazaar and planned their work without consulting you?' And he showed me things in the article . . . harsh criticisms which were the fruit of weariness and worry, and which never would have been penned in the calm of communion with Christ.

Robert never forgot that day and its deep influence on his life was often seen. People frequently felt the presence of Christ himself when talking with him. One friend wrote, 'It was impossible to come into your room without knowing Christ was there too. And somehow the whole day became calm and joyous after talking with you.'

Bitter Disappointment

But a severe disappointment was to strike. Constant overwork and exhaustion coupled with the relentless Indian climate finally led to a severe breakdown. Early in 1902 his doctor ordered some weeks' rest in Switzerland to see if the more bracing air would help. Weeks passed and he felt no stronger. Eventually he had to face the fact that he must give up his much-loved work in India. Helene packed up their home single-handed, caring for their four little girls, all under seven, on the sea voyage to join him. Robert's mother, Eliza Jane Wilder, now aged eighty, travelled with them.

It was hard not to feel keenly discouraged. What would the future hold? Was this to be the end of all he had prepared and worked for? Month after month he failed to regain the strength for which he longed. All he could do was to cry out to God in his uncertainty and weakness. Robert's prayer at this time was that he might be 'constantly and completely within the circle of God's will'. Even in the midst of feeling so low he was able to write, 'Rest comes only in being yoked with the Burden Bearer. His yoke is easy. His burden light.'

And their heavenly Father *did* continue to care for them. They were able to stay in a welcoming Christian guest house in Vevey on lovely Lake Geneva, with the beauty of the rugged Dent de Jaman in the distance. That winter Hudson Taylor, now an old man in his seventieth year, joined them in the guest house. Their times of fellowship together tremendously encouraged the

Wilders. As a young man, Hudson Taylor had founded the China Inland Mission, which grew to over 1,000 missionaries and had the goal of planting Christian churches in even the remotest provinces of China. But after thirty-five years of strenuous and sacrificial work, the horrendous Boxer Rising of 1900 threatened to crush the new churches and eliminate the missionaries. Letter after letter arrived recounting the tortures and martyrdoms taking place in China. Hudson Taylor was still reeling from successive blows. So Robert, still weak although in his early forties, and the elderly missionary pioneer encouraged one another.

When spring came the Wilder family returned to their peaceful home in Veldre, Norway; and here at last Robert's strength began slowly to return.

A New Challenge

In the autumn of 1904, after nearly two years of 'uselessness', God's new plans began to unfold. Although Robert's heart was set on overseas mission, God knew he would fulfil a far more strategic role in challenging others to go. This would multiply his effectiveness. Under God's hand, he found that disappointment could lead to fresh opportunities. Tissington Tatlow, leader of the Student Christian Movement in Britain, which had developed out of the SVM, invited Robert to make a short tour of the British universities. Travelling widely, he was greatly encouraged to see the growth of missionary interest. Thirteen years earlier, when he had presided at the conference in Edinburgh, some two hundred had become volunteers. Now there were over 2,000, of whom many were already overseas. Later that year Robert was invited to join the SCM staff, and he worked for them in a variety of roles for thirteen happy years. His constant aim was to deepen the students' spiritual lives and to challenge hundreds more to sacrifice for the sake of a world which still did not know Christ as Saviour and Lord.

Helene was now able to play a more prominent part beside him as they opened their home to many students. She loved home-making, and with her practical gifts and easy manner soon made visitors feel at ease. Sundays were especially 'open house' and the Wilder girls enjoyed the lively international company.

During these years, Stanley Hoyte, a medical student in London, heard Robert Wilder speak and came to respect him deeply, both as a person and for his teaching. Frequently he visited the Wilder home. Stanley Hoyte was to be my father.

Robert was still not strong when he started work with the SCM; he and Helene depended very much on prayer. Each term they would circulate their friends with a prayer card, listing Robert's commitments. They urged them strongly to pray *daily*. Right from the early days with his sister Grace, Robert had discovered the power of prayer to change people and situations. He now grew to depend on it more and more. 'He that saveth time from prayer', he would say, 'shall lose it. But he that loseth time waiting on God shall find it in blessing others.'

To illustrate the power of prayer he used to relate the story of a Norwegian country woman he met on his first walking tour. As they chatted, he asked her to pray that the British SVM would come into being. Ten years later he met her again. Recognizing him, she insisted he come into her simple home. Gathering her family round, she asked Robert to tell them how her prayers had been answered. 'It may be,' he concluded, 'that woman through her ministry of prayer did more towards bringing the British SVM into being than any of us travelling secretaries.'

In the messages he gave Robert shared from his own experience the joy and privilege of prayer and stressed the importance of reading the Bible each day so as to discern the will of God. His aim was to deepen the students' personal relationship with God and his favourite topic was the Holy Spirit and the difference he can make in a life fully surrendered to him. Often the Bible studies he led were on the early chapters of Acts, drawing out lessons relevant to his student audience. Some of the talks he gave

were on 'Spiritual Power and Missions', 'The Uniqueness of
Christ' and 'Sainthood for the Sake of Others'. His message was
always simple and direct. He made no claim to oratory. 'One felt
the old gospel has still the power to attract and help, even though
presented in a very ordinary way,' he recorded. Others recalled
how, 'his charm of manner absolutely held his audience' and how
'they speak of your message as one of the most inspiring things
in their memory. God certainly was wonderfully using you.'

Robert gave himself freely in friendship and hospitality to the
students. 'The extraordinary lovingkindness of the man' impressed one of his colleagues. Yet his love did not lack courage.
'I saw it in your eyes that you would help me ruthlessly,' another
one wrote who later served God for many years in the Balkans.
Robert had a keen sense of humour and loved jokes. His friendly
blue eyes would twinkle with fun as he listened to some new
story. He always had plenty of anecdotes from his own wide
experience to liven up a social gathering. Many were drawn to
his company and his home for the friendly atmosphere of
spontaneity they found there. Yet this was the man who had
been brought up under the shadow of a dominating father who
had antagonized so many. By God's grace he had profited from
the positives of his upbringing – the total dedication to Christ
and to the goal of world-wide mission. At the same time God's
grace had counteracted the negatives, enabling him to replace
hostility and self-righteousness with beautiful relationships.

Helene's Important Role

During these years when the Wilder family was based in
England, Helene took their four daughters to Norway each
summer to maintain their Scandinavian heritage. Leaving in
early May, they missed the summer term, and so took all their
school books with them. All morning they would study under
the strict supervision of Tante Aagot, their mother's older sister.

Then they would be free to enjoy the delights of mountain, lake and forest, and the wide network of relatives who lived nearby.

A few months ago I caught the stopping train from Oslo going north, and tried to picture the excitement the children would have felt as they returned to their much-loved homeland. Each curve of the line brought fresh glimpses of rolling hills, green forests and little red wooden homesteads trimmed with white paint. One moment we passed a tumbling brook, the next we entered a wide valley with sleek cows contentedly grazing. How each familiar landmark must have raised their level of anticipation, until the train carrying the little family finally chugged into Veldre station.

'Norheim' was a wonderful rambling white wooden house, to which several additional rooms had been added over the years as they were needed. Here, as in every home she created, Helene's warm personality made her the centre of the community. She managed everything with quiet efficiency, hiring helpers and arranging for any necessary repairs. Robert, who was not at all practical, was spared the demands of the daily routine. They had some faithful helpers who lived nearby. They all enjoyed working at 'Norheim', as they were never treated like 'servants' but always as the friends they really were.

The biggest excitement came when Robert was due to arrive after some long journey. The house, always spotless, was given an extra shine. Tante Aagot would fill the rooms with flowers. The American flag was hoisted to the top of the flag-pole, and tiny Norwegian flags were placed along the path leading to the gate. The girls would run down to the station and wait for the train to come puffing in, and give their father a great welcome. His luggage would then be piled on to a hand-cart, to be brought up later, and the laughing, chattering group would walk up the hill to the house. The whole household took on a new life and interest, as Robert, a gifted story-teller, recounted his recent travels.

The daughters remembered that there were always visitors at 'Norheim'. They were taught how to take care of them and enjoy them. Three of Helene's nieces thought of 'Norheim'as their second home. Students whom Robert had met on his travels often came to stay. And each year two special bachelor friends arrived. One was Baron Paul Nicolay, the founder of the Russian SCM, a gentle, fun-loving man, who persevered with the student work in spite of many difficulties. The other was Count Joachim Moltke, whom Robert had met in 1891 on his first visit to Denmark. They had talked until long after midnight after one of his meetings. But his hostess, who reckoned she knew the young Count well, laughed at the thought of his showing interest. She promptly informed Robert of the 'worldly-minded ways' of this elegant and wealthy young man. Much taken aback, Robert wondered if he had made a mistake speaking with him as he had. But Count Moltke was soon captivated for God and spent a life-time supporting missions. Robert had humbly to ask God's forgiveness for the lack of faith shown in his reaction to his hostess's remarks. From this episode he learnt never to pre-judge anyone.

Robert loved the peace and quiet of 'Norheim'. His children remembered often seeing him walking alone in the garden early in the morning, with his New Testament in his hand. This was his favourite way of communing with God. After breakfast he would gather everyone for family prayers, friends and helpers alike, Count sitting next to gardener. It could be a lengthy affair, as Robert loved expounding the Scriptures and the family enjoyed singing together.

Family Traditions

Robert and Helene both knew the importance of strong family ties and invested much time and thought in building delightful family traditions. Sunday was planned to be a special day so that the girls would look forward to it. 'Coffee in bed!' would come

Severine's cheery call from the kitchen. She would mount the stairs with a tray of home-baked cookies and fresh raspberry juice if you were too young for coffee. A leisurely breakfast would follow, ham omelettes and newly-baked rye bread. There would always be fresh flowers on the table arranged by Tante Aagot. Then the family would walk the half-hour to church together, past farms and stretches of woodland. Sunday dinner was always special, particularly the rich desserts which Severine was skilled at producing, so that the only thing to do afterwards was to enjoy a long siesta in the hammock, swinging gently in the shade of the silver birches. Late afternoon coffee was served outside, accompanied by delicious crisp waffles and other home-baked cookies. Then the whole family would go for a walk, sometimes down to the lake for a freezing cold swim and sometimes over to a beautiful viewpoint.

The day would be rounded off by hymn singing and a simple supper. Everyone, young and old, was expected to recite a favourite Bible verse and choose a hymn. They were all very musical and greatly enjoyed these times together.

Robert's birthday in August became the highlight of the year when all the Norwegian cousins would gather at 'Norheim'. There would be news to catch up on and games to be played in the garden. Afternoon coffee would be served, together with *kringle* (a rich coffee cake in the shape of an initial) and sugared waffles and *blot kake* (filled and iced cake).

Reading Aunt Ruth's account of her happy childhood made me realize what a rich heritage my mother and her sisters received. In spite of their many moves, this gave them a solid foundation and a model on which they could build in later life.

Wider Ministry

Under God's gracious hand, Robert Wilder's gifts and personality were to be used even more widely. In 1895 his life-long friend

John Mott set out for an epic journey to unite all student Christian groups around the globe into the World Student Christian Federation. The journey took nearly two years and brought him and his wife to Europe, Ceylon, India, Australia, China, Japan and Hawaii. As we have seen, several of these national movements came into existence through Robert Wilder's vision, and he was often invited to visit them. Based in England, he frequently travelled through Scandinavia, where his fluency in Norwegian made it easy for the students to confide in him. He was much encouraged and humbled by the way God used him there.

In 1911 the ninth conference of the World Student Christian Federation was held at Robert College, Constantinople (Istanbul). The college had been founded by Royal Wilder's friend, Christopher Robert, after whom Robert himself had been named. On the long journey across Europe 'word came along the corridor that Wilder was on the train', a Scottish delegate recalled. 'I went along to see him, and found him cheerful and tranquil as always . . . Later on I saw him deep in talk with a Jewish businessman. "What's he up to now?" I said to one of my companions. "He's out for souls!" said she. So it proved. The stranger had opened his mind . . . The gulf between them had been crossed by sympathy and sincerity.'

Robert gave the final address of the conference, challenging the delegates with a characteristic phrase: 'The question is not whether the age of miracles is past, but whether the age of faith is past.'

From Constantinople he set off for a six weeks tour of universities in Hungary and Austria, where there was as yet no Christian student work. In six major Hungarian cities he was given the opportunity to lecture and new branches of the Student Christian Movement began to spring up. Robert's knowledge of German was a great help in personal interviews, although he needed an interpreter for larger meetings. When searching for a common language with which to communicate with the secretary of one of the newly formed groups, they resorted to New Testament Greek, and thus carried on an extensive correspondence over the years!

He found Vienna, a city of 10,000 students, split by racial bitterness between Germans and Slavs; there was strong opposition from Jews and atheists to the Roman Catholic dominance. He met with ten picked professors for three and a half hours, and discussed the possibility of forming a Christian Union among the students. The majority were very sceptical, but finally one remarked that if religion could succeed in uniting the different races, 'it will do what military and political organizations have failed to accomplish.'

In the opening meeting Robert's interpreter failed him and one of the professors took his place. Most of the audience considered religion to be synonymous with a closed mind because of the legalistic clericalism around them. 'It seemed a new thing to have Christ proclaimed as a living reality, able in our day to save men from sin,' Robert recorded. When he left, a small group had formed – Germans, Czechs, Magyars and Ruthenians. They told him, 'The secret of your wonderful influence is that you think, and speak and do, all and always in the spirit of love.'

Aware of hostile feelings between Czechs and Germans in Prague and of the strong mood of agnosticism there, Robert wondered what sort of reception he would be given. However, spontaneous applause broke out at the end of his first lecture and more than half the audience stayed behind for an after-meeting. Twenty-one students formed the core of the new group who waved him goodbye.

The following spring Robert visited Holland, with meetings in Wageningen and Utrecht. From there he journeyed to Marseilles, Montauban and Paris. Three weeks in Italy followed, speaking in the universities of Naples, Rome, Perugia and Bologna, and finally he spent four days in Austria at the University of Graz. In each place he divided his time between the larger

meetings and private talks, often feeling, as usual, that the latter
were of more strategic value. He commented on Montauban,
'From 10 a.m. until 12.30 at night I was barely alone one hour.'

Graz was the most difficult. Racial feuds and religious apathy,
coupled with a threatened boycott of the meeting and the
difficulty of obtaining police permission to hold it, presented
huge problems. From the twenty-two who turned up a small
group decided to form a Christian Union. Although all were
nominally Roman Catholic, none of them possessed a Bible. So
after providing them with New Testaments, Robert launched
them on the study of Mark's Gospel.

Such extensive travel in noisy, sooty steam trains must have
been tedious and exhausting, while the many different languages
made communication difficult.

1913 saw Robert Wilder back in Eastern Europe, visiting the
two Bohemian centres of Prague and Brunn and the Polish
universities of Krakow and Lemberg. His meetings seldom lasted
less than three and a half hours but many hundreds of students
came, although they often had to stand the whole time. The need
for training leaders became increasingly apparent, and a meeting
to discuss this was held in Perau. The manager of the hotel was
amazed to see the mixture of Protestants and Roman Catholics,
of Poles, Germans, Czechs and Magyars all enjoying each other's
company. Robert had the knack of reaching right across racial
and cultural boundaries. One student remarked, 'You have the
gift of appealing to the Slavic and eastern mind which few
westerners have.'

'Where did this amazing gift spring from?' I wondered as I
read his story again. Then it dawned on me that this too began
with his youthful struggles when he was wrenched from familiar
Indian life and thrown into the totally different culture of
America. Those teenage years had not been easy. But they taught
him flexibility and adaptability, making him sensitive to very
different types of people. God was able to use him in a special
way because of this.

1914 brought further opportunities in Switzerland, Vienna, Zagreb and Belgrade. From there he spent twelve days in Turkey, and then travelled on to Bulgaria. In Sofia he spoke to over a thousand students on 'Moral Atrophy and the Regeneration of Society'. (Interestingly, my husband has recently spoken several times on similar themes in Eastern Europe.) Robert's tour finished in the universities of Oporto, Lisbon and Coimbra in Portugal. When one considers how slow travel was in those days and how primitive the railways, it is remarkable how he was given strength for so much.

God led him to buy a house in the mountains of Silesia as a much-needed Bible school and conference centre. On this last tour Robert had the joy of attending the first conference there with delegates from all over Austria and Hungary. 'Like oil spread over troubled waters came the address by Dr. Wilder on Easter Sunday,' one man recalled. But that year Europe smouldered like a threatening volcano. War was soon to break out, putting an end to these travels.

Return to America

During the first world war Britain experienced increasing financial pressure; Robert Wilder resigned from the SCM to spare the movement from having to raise his salary. For a year he enjoyed quiet refreshment in his peaceful home in Norway. Then another invitation from John Mott brought him back to the work of the YMCA in America. A few years later another invitation drew him back to his 'first love', to become General Secretary of the American Student Volunteer Movement. 'The evangelization of the world in this generation' had been the driving force of his life for many years, governing every major decision. Again he was encouraged by its motivating power in the lives of students, and even more so now, as a new generation of dedicated and effective leaders was emerging.

It is interesting to compare the two close friends, John Mott and Robert Wilder. They had known each other since student days and deeply valued their relationship and each other's advice. But unlike Mott, who was a well-known mission executive, Wilder was essentially a grass-roots missionary, who was often overseas when major conferences took place. Robert did not achieve fame through prolific writing, as did some others; indeed he found writing a laborious chore, interfering with more urgent missionary tasks. Robert's gentle, self-effacing manner made him shun public acclaim. He preferred hands-on ministry to board-room influence. It has been said that 'Wilder grasped better than most of his contemporaries the real essence of servanthood and discipleship.'

In the first five-year period under his renewed leadership more new volunteers sailed than ever before. The encouragements were great but the task of raising sufficient funds for them all was immense. 'Prayer and hard work' formed his answer.

But during this post-war period a new atmosphere became apparent among the students. The horrendous waste of human life which had just taken place, coupled with a severe world recession, turned their thoughts towards political and social issues. Some became impatient toward those foreign missions which aimed at the transformation of individual lives without looking at the needs of society. Others were influenced by the growth of liberal theology and cast doubts on the Bible as a practical guide for daily living. At the same time students were demanding a larger share in the running of the movement. Many who felt international peace to be the urgent need of that time, rather than world-wide evangelism, were unaware that mission attitudes were actually changing, abandoning an assumption of western superiority and moving towards the inclusion of social concerns alongside evangelism.

These struggles taxed his leadership skills greatly, especially as the generation gap between him and the students grew wider. But remembering the beginnings of the movement, Robert trusted in prayer and in giving the students their head. At the same time, he continually attempted to maintain the emphasis on evangelism. 'Whether a man (*sic*) goes out as an agricultural missionary or as a medical missionary, all the work in the strictest sense of the term should be evangelistic,' he urged, refusing to compromise on the original vision. He found himself engaged in a difficult battle, intensified as many also began questioning the relationship between Christianity and other faiths. He appears to have grown increasingly disappointed with the new direction the SVM was taking, and in 1927 he resigned. Unlike his father, in a similar situation, Robert was able to resign with no ill will on either side.

Ministry in the Middle East

The final ministry to which God called Robert Wilder took him in a new direction, and yet drew on the many valuable gifts he had been developing. At the age of 65 he was asked to become Executive Secretary for the Near East Christian Council. His area of responsibility extended from Morocco on the west to Iran on the east and from the Balkan countries and Turkey in the north to Arabia, Abyssinia and Sudan in the south. Approximately 2,000 Protestant missionaries worked in this area, representing over a hundred different missionary societies, many of whom held opposing theologies. To draw them together in closer fellowship and co-operation was not going to be easy. But Robert was used to crossing denominational boundaries. And his own rich mission experience and familiarity with the workings of committees fitted him in a unique way for this task.

Knowing that they were about to make their home where French was the official language, Robert and Helene worked on improving their fluency. He described to a friend their daily routine: 'In the morning we read together a chapter from the Old Testament in Norwegian, pray together in English, and then she reads from the French New Testament in order that we may brush it up . . . After breakfast we have prayers in Norwegian after we have sung a Swedish hymn. . . . There is every inducement in Europe to be a polyglot.'

The doctor was concerned about Robert's limited strength and advised that as they were planning to live in Cairo, they should return each summer to the cooler climate of Norway. Aware of his increasing physical weakness, Robert looked more and more to communion with God to give him strength. He decided to tithe his time, giving this tithe to prayer. 'It does make a difference,' he wrote to a friend. 'I try to give one and a half hours before breakfast and the last hour I give before the evening meal. Sometimes one has to be firm with one's friends. When driving with a missionary recently I said, "The time has come for communion with the Master. Do you mind if we drive in silence?" Strangely enough she didn't resent it . . . and certainly her silent communion with God was worth infinitely more than anything I could have said.'

Wishing to see for himself something of his area of responsibility before settling down in Cairo, Robert travelled there overland from Greece. In Athens the international training school for leaders impressed him with its potential. More than half the students came after his lecture to talk personally. Continuing his journey by sea, he visited Constantinople, where he spoke to college students, national leaders and missionaries from across the spectrum – Greek Orthodox, Armenian and Protestant churches. Two nights by train brought him to Aleppo, from where he travelled by car 630 miles over the Lebanese mountains, along the shore of the Mediterranean and through beautiful valleys. Among those he met were many old friends he had known as students in Britain or America.

Motoring into Palestine, he commented, 'How real the Gospels became as we looked over the places where Christ healed and spoke.' In Jerusalem he preached in the cathedral

and the YMCA, visiting mission schools and hospitals. Finally
he travelled on to Port Said to be reunited with Helene and his
youngest daughter, who had come by ship from Norway.

Six very full years followed. Robert and Helene called them
'some of our happiest years'. Their great desire was to create a
spirit of unity, transcending theological and ecclesiastical differences. This was not easy in a work where Christian co-operation
was a new idea and many of the missionaries were strong
individuals with tenacious beliefs. The chairman of the Council
wrote later of Robert's work: 'Wherever you have gone suspi-
cion has vanished, lack of faith in the project has disappeared,
and a new reality has been given to Jesus' prayer, "that they might
be one". Moreover, you have done this without sacrificing any
of your own personal viewpoints or essential doctrine.' Robert
himself wrote:

> 'To me, Jesus Christ means everything. . . . I have attained the
> certitude of being in connection with Christ (through) a careful
> study of the New Testament, contact with intimate friends . . .
> to whom Christ was a great reality . . . and my own personal
> experience. At first I believed in him merely with the faith of
> authority, but through prayer I came to a personal faith when he
> became real to me . . . I should sooner lose everything than the
> friendship and fellowship of Christ.'

Thanks to a very capable secretary in Cairo and Helene's unsel-
fishness and competent home-making, Robert was able to travel
widely throughout the Near East. Often the journeys were
difficult and dangerous, such as when he was driven from Mosul
in Iraq to Nebk in Syria, over roads made almost impassable by
heavy rain. Conversation proved difficult. Having discovered
that the other passenger, a Chaldean, could understand his
German, Robert asked him to translate into Turkish for the
Armenian driver. Delayed by a puncture, they finally reached
Deir-ez-zar, only to find the missionaries were away. The next

day the rain poured down and they were caught in a bog for
nearly two hours. 'Every effort to get the car to move was futile.
. . . At last a truck came along the lonely road and two men from
it helped us get out of the bog . . . they nearly gave up until I
promised baksheesh. I did not like the thought of spending the
night in the wilderness . . .'. When they finally reached Nebk
the following day they heard that only five days earlier a car
making the same trip had been bogged down all night and
attacked by wolves! One man had died and another was seriously
hurt. How Robert thanked God for bringing them safely
through!

A high point for him was a six week tour of Persia [Iran]:
'2,000 miles by car, over roads that were in places indescribably
rough, whizzing round hairpin curves, gliding past precipices and
over mountain passes, some of which were over 8,000 feet in
height'. By God's grace, he never missed a single appointment,
and was given strength to speak at numerous meetings. In
Teheran he spoke ten times in three days. He met many fine
Persian Christians and called it 'one of the most hopeful Muslim
fields in the world'. He was especially moved by some recent
converts – one the son of a head mullah, another whose own
brother had signed his death warrant and who had only just
managed to escape. He rejoiced to find Armenians, Nestorians,
Jewish and Muslim converts all worshipping God together. In
later years of fierce persecution under the Ayatollah Khomeini,
these solid foundations kept the church strong. So this thoroughly indigenous movement of God greatly encouraged
Robert.

Robert often stressed the necessity for all Christians to be
filled with the Holy Spirit. He taught that this was both a crisis
and a process, and was essential for every type of ministry.
Although he never became a Pentecostal, he found his Presbyterian roots too restrictive, and rejoiced when others moved
into a greater freedom in their spiritual lives. Constantly he

aimed at deepening the spiritual tone of the missionary teams, stressing 'Christ-controlled service'.

However, the incessant travel over long and difficult roads took its toll. The constant giving out to others would have drained the energy of a man much younger than himself. On returning from a visit to Sudan, Robert fell seriously ill. In spite of months of rest and medical care he could not muster strength to recover. In 1933, when Robert was in his seventieth year, he and Helene left for retirement in Norway. The members of the Near East Christian Council expressed their sense of loss and yet of deep appreciation in the following words:

> 'His messages, and yet more his very personality, have made God seem real and near. His faith has helped to kindle and keep burning the hope for the coming of Christ's kingdom. . . . His labours among our Missions, his unwearying travels from country to country, his patience with our limitations and slowness of progress, and the wisdom of his counsels have won our highest admiration and our deepest gratitude'.

Five more years still remained to him. Time for Robert and Helene to rest and relax together in the beauties of Norway. Time to come closer to the Lord they loved. Time to minister again among students as limited strength allowed. And time to write out of the rich experience of the past. Some of Robert's books and pamphlets were translated into many different languages.

In both 1934 and 1935 he was back in Britain, now at the invitation of the Inter Varsity Fellowship. This younger group had broken away from the SCM (see page 58 above). Subsequently the influence of the IVF (now UCCF) increased in Britain, and the SCM diminished, so that now it is only a publishing house. Robert and Helene deeply regretted the division caused by the existence of two rival organizations. But they understood the reasons, and felt that IVF now represented

their original ideals more closely than SCM. But they wished
to bring the two groups closer together. Robert's entire Christian service had been spent in co-operative, international and
inter-denominational enterprises. He had always stood for unity
of the Spirit among Christians. Those who were close to him
as he grew more elderly were impressed by his saintliness, his
gentle spirit of love for all fellow Christians, and his devotion
to Christ.

Earlier in 1934, Robert and Helene's daughter, Grace, a
missionary in far away China, gave birth to her sixth child, who
was to be author of this book.

In their prayer life, Robert and Helene still continued to roam
the world. But they were now content to live quietly at 'Norheim', enjoying their many friends and relations and the lovely
countryside. His feelings are expressed in a poem he loved to
quote:

> And so I am watching quietly every day.
> Whenever the sun shines brightly I rise and say,
> 'Surely it is the shining of His face,'
> And I look unto the gates of his high place beyond the sea,
> For I know He is coming shortly to summon me.
> And when a shadow falls across the window of my room,
> Where I am working my appointed task,
> I lift my head to watch the door and ask,
> If He is come.
> And the angel answers sweetly in my home –
> Only a few more shadows, and He will come.

So it was that one day in 1938 the Lord took Robert Wilder
home. Letters from all around the world poured in to comfort
Helene, his much-loved companion for forty-five years. They
spoke of the blessing hundreds had received, in four continents,
through the life of this one who had put himself entirely at his
Lord's disposal.

BIBLIOGRAPHY
for Chapters 3 & 4

Braisted, Ruth Wilder, *In this Generation: The Story of Robert P. Wilder* (New York: Friendship Press, 1941).

—'Norheim': *Memories of Childhood* (unpublished, 1975).

Hopkins, Howard C., *John R. Mott (1865–1955): A Biography* (Grand Rapids: Eerdmans, 1979).

Johnson, Douglas, *Contending for the Faith: A History of the Evangelical Movement in the Universities and Colleges* (Nottingham: IVP, 1979).

Mott, John R., *Five Decades and a Forward View* (New York/London: Harper, 1939).

Patterson, James A., *The Legacy of Robert P. Wilder* (International Bulletin of Missionary Research, January 1991).

Rouse, Ruth and Neill, Stephen Charles, *A History of the Ecumenical Movement 1517–1948* (London: SPCK, 1954).

Tatlow, Tissington, *The Story of the Student Christian Movement of Great Britain and Northern Ireland* (London: SCM, 1933).

Wilder, Robert P., *The Perils and Privileges of the Student Volunteer Movement* (Address given in 1891).

—*The Great Commission* (Edinburgh: Oliphants, 1936).

—*The Student Volunteer Movement for Foreign Missions: Some Personal Reminiscences of its Origin and Early History* (New York: SVM, 1935).

Chapter 5

Surgeon to Five Million People

Travel in Inland China

At the time when Robert Wilder was busy encouraging Christian fellowships in the universities of Eastern Europe, before the first World War shattered the peace, one of his missionary volunteers was making his way across China to his first mission station after language school. Inland China was unbelievably primitive in those days. Only a few railways had been built, so travel was restricted to the same methods as had been followed for centuries. One could either trudge the long miles on foot, or be jolted in a wheelbarrow, or, if funds were sufficient, one could ride a donkey for part of the way. The distant city of Linfen lay ten weeks' journey from the coast. If a church could be found in the towns or villages on the way, the traveller would find a ready welcome: plenty of hot water, and a clean brick *kang* to sleep on, heated by a warm fire. But more often the local inn provided the only available accommodation: crowded and noisy, and infested with fleas and bed-bugs.

Dr. Stanley Hoyte was a young English surgeon, tall and athletic, who had won two silver cups for long-distance running in the London inter-hospital sports. He had a zest for life and fun which made him take a keen interest in all around him. As a gifted pianist, with a keen appreciation of music and art, he must have been moved by the poverty and dreary conditions. A few years later he wrote, 'Everywhere one sees crumbling walls, roads mere cart-tracks, houses dark and dirty, streets smelly and physical life unclean and (unless forced to labour for a living) inactive.

And above all, mental life stolid and seemingly overshadowed by a dense fog.' The widespread addiction to opium accounted for much of the mental inertia, which stood in marked contrast to the glories of a rich cultural heritage which was already well established in China when Christ came to earth. But trapped as she was for centuries by her ancient traditions and cutting herself off from all outside 'barbarian' influence, China desperately needed the message of God's love.

New Freedom in the Churches

Stan, as he was known to his friends, came from a close Christian family of nine brothers and sisters. His father had taken the bold step of breaking with the traditional religiosity of his day. Much of Anglicanism had grown cold and formal: the 'High-Church' influence was spreading a greater emphasis on rituals and vestments, and the 'priestly' functions of the minister. At the same time liberal theology was beginning to undermine faith in the Bible as the inspired word of God and the Christian's all-sufficient guide. John Henry Newman (1801–90), one of the leaders of this Anglo-Catholic movement, had taken the next logical step and in 1845 abandoned Anglicanism for Roman Catholicism. But his younger brother, Francis William Newman, turned his eyes in a different direction.

During the 1820s, groups of Christians who studied the Bible carefully began to ask why the church needed an ordained ministry at all. In the New Testament they read about Christians 'breaking bread in their homes and eating together with glad and sincere hearts' (Acts 2:46), apparently quite uninhibited by whether there was a priest present or not. Led by men like Anthony Norris Groves and J. N. Darby, Francis William Newman and many others began to do the same. As some of the leaders were based in Plymouth, they became known as Plymouth Brethren.

Stan's father had found a welcome new spiritual vitality in these informal groups which contrasted strongly with the traditionalism of his Anglican church. In the new 'assemblies' every believer was reckoned to have the Holy Spirit of Christ and therefore to be able to teach and pray. There were no full-time ministers: all were to be involved in ministry, and the warmth and love which was felt between them was infectious.

It is never easy to make a break with the past and William Henry Hoyte, Stan's father, probably faced much antagonism and misunderstanding. But his action led to the establishment of a home where God was honoured and loved, and where the Bible set the guide-lines for all their decisions. Two of his sons became missionary doctors – Julyan in Zambia and Stanley in China – and one of his daughters, Florence, served as a missionary for many years in India. At the time of writing Florence is still alive, and at the age of 110 is one of the oldest people in Britain.

William Henry Hoyte could trace his ancestry back to 1681 when a certain John Hoyte was born. He served the Duke of Rutland for fifty years as his game-keeper at Belvoir Castle. Five generations of the family worked for successive dukes, and some left fascinating accounts of their times. The aristocratic look of William Henry's Aunt Bella seemed to distinguish her from the rest of the Hoytes. Her garrulous younger sister, Sophie, would give a knowing look and remark, 'If you look at some of the portraits in Belvoir Castle you'll see where Bella gets her features from!'

A Christian Heritage

Stan's mother's side of the family had not reacted so strongly against ritualism. She liked to tell her children of her two great-aunts, Ann and Susan, who lived together as spinsters in Reading, and spent their days caring for others. They had four spare bedrooms, and would frequently invite over-pressed clergy wives to come for a rest and a break from the demands of the vicarage. Living very simply themselves, they had worked out a most unusual way of caring for the needy. Every day two poor widows were invited to eat dinner in the kitchen with the maids. To finish up the ample left-overs, two orphans were also fed in the scullery. It is an interesting cameo – maintaining the class-conscious decorum of those days, and yet giving twelve needy women a good meal once a week, and reaching out to orphans too!

In 1878 the first tramway in Reading was being constructed outside their home. These two maiden aunts bustled to and prepared some food and a big cauldron of cocoa for the workmen at the end of the day. Explaining their actions they said, 'With something warm inside them they may go straight home to their families, instead of drinking all night in the pub!' Interestingly, Aunt Ann and Aunt Susan attended Greyfriars Church in Reading. Nearly a hundred years later I came to Reading to lecture at the Polytechnic, and Greyfriars was the church which commended me for missionary service.

So Stan grew up in the love and security of a Christian family. His father appeared a trifle distant at times as he was very engrossed in developing his business. With the industrial revolution at its height, there were many needy working-class people near him in Nottingham, and he designed and built affordable homes for them. A century later some of these can be found within the slums of Nottingham: but at the time they provided just the housing required. Stan's mother often shielded her husband from the noise and bustle of the growing family. A warm, loving and capable woman, she kept the large household running smoothly and efficiently.

One of Stan's treats as a child was to go by train with a brother or sister to the little village of Whatstandwell in Derbyshire to stay with their Granny. His sister Frances described her as 'a little old lady with rather a crumpled face and a whimsical smile, and when one kissed her, such a soft skin. She always wore a high

lace cap, a plain one in the morning, and a pretty one in the
afternoon, trimmed with little bunches of black velvet ribbon.
She describes the house as having 'fantastic views across the
Derwent valley, and a steep garden with paths and steps and a
lovely stream running in a series of pools to a waterfall. . . . At
night Granny always tucked us up in bed, and gave us a "pillow".
A "pillow" was a good-night text. And I can see her now saying,
"Underneath are the everlasting arms", or "[God] giveth his
beloved sleep". We would snuggle down in the big double bed,
with its canopy and chintz curtains, feeling loved and "done-to"
(i.e. well looked-after) – her own expression.'

Stan was grateful for this Christian upbringing, but there were
some things about the Plymouth Brethren which he struggled
against. In attempting to pattern all their structures and worship
styles on the New Testament church, they refused their women
equal status with the men. Stan felt they had sadly misread Paul's
teaching on the subject; and in later life wrote long and full
articles pleading with them to see things differently. He also
found the Brethren rather exclusive, welcoming Christians only
from other recognized assemblies of the Brethren. Their missionaries, too, were unwilling to join any of the recognized
missionary societies. Stan loved to welcome all who loved the
Lord Jesus as brothers and sisters in Christ. So he offered his
services to the China Inland Mission, a society which embraced
people from all walks of life and all types of churches.

I am not sure when he developed this wider view of the
Church of God. I wonder whether it was during his medical
studies in London, when in the hospital Christian Union he was
rubbing shoulders with Christians from all denominations. Might
it also have been when he visited the home of Robert Wilder
on Hampstead Heath, and found his horizons stretched and his
heart warmed by the personality of that godly man? Little did he
realize then that he would marry one of Robert Wilder's
daughters. Even less would he have guessed that a child of that
marriage would write about him more than eighty years later.

I remember Father telling me about his impressions attending the Edinburgh Mission Conference of 1910 as a young doctor aged twenty-five. Sitting down to meals together, the delegates were amazed to find that their unity in Christ bridged the gap between the denominations. Many of them had never related to an Anglican or Methodist or Baptist. Some had tears in their eyes as, for the first time, they embraced people from other denominations who they now realized were united in the same goal of taking Christ to the nations of the world. This unity on fundamentals was to be one of the foundational principles of Father's life. It is so easy today to take this mutual acceptance for granted, but many of Father's generation had to struggle for it.

CIM hospital in Linfen

After weeks of arduous travel, Father reached the wide plains of central Shansi (or Shanxi) province, in the north of China, to the south west of Beijing. Here he was due to assist Dr. John Carr in the mission hospital in Linfen. Medical work has frequently played a key part in the modern missionary movement. In spite of Rufus Anderson's earlier plea that the missionary's sole task should be evangelism, the desirability of caring for people's bodies as well as their 'souls' was obvious. When William Carey sailed for India his only colleague was a medical man. Dr. William Lockhart, as the first Protestant missionary in North China, found it was only by offering medical treatment that he could gain a hearing for the gospel. Fifty years later, when Father arrived in China, medical knowledge had increased greatly and had become an effective resource in the hands of those who for love of Christ were willing to sacrifice lucrative prospects in their homeland.

The church in Shansi had seen remarkable growth twenty years before Father arrived, partly due to the able leadership of a converted Confucian scholar who had been an opium addict. Because of his dependence on opium, Pastor Hsi, as he came to be known, had been a complete wreck, with his finances exhausted and his marriage on the rocks. But God had healed him in a remarkable way. In gratitude he started opium refuges all over southern Shansi, extending into neighbouring provinces. Through his work hundreds of addicts were converted and Christian families established all over the area.

But soon after Pastor Hsi died tragedy had struck the newly developing churches. A strong anti-foreign feeling had been smouldering for some years, fuelled by anger at the way western powers forced themselves on China, annexing port after port. Three years of famine lit the fuse. In June 1900 the wily Empress Dowager seized her opportunity and issued an imperial edict ordering the killing of all foreigners within her kingdom. Her trusted agents were a secret society, nick-named 'the Boxers', deeply steeped in occult Taoism, who practised mysticism and trances to make themselves invincible to sword and bullet. Joined by 8,000 troops, they stormed through the countryside, hunting down and killing all foreign missionaries and their Chinese converts.

The Governor of Shansi worked hand in glove with the Empress Dowager and personally supervised the massacre of Chinese Christians by the hundreds and the torture and death of many missionaries. Out of 188 foreigners killed in China at this time, 159 died in Shansi. A few missionaries attempted to escape overland through Honan. They endured a terrible thousand-mile journey in the blistering heat of July and August, mostly on foot, tormented by the local population, and in an almost starving and naked condition. Some of them died on the way. Dr. Millar Wilson of Linfen was among those martyred for Christ. The hospital to which Father was appointed was named after him.

With the suppression of the Boxers, China had been left in turmoil. The Empress Dowager soon lost her power and died in 1908, leaving the four year old Pu-Yi on the throne. Many today know his sad story through the striking film, 'The Last Emperor'. 1911 saw the overthrow of the Manchu dynasty who had ruled the nation since 1644, vainly attempting to maintain their policy of cultural isolation. The doors of China were then thrown open to foreigners in a way not known before. But for the next four decades that tragic country was to be torn by civil war, one revolutionary power vying with another to gain overall control.

It was into this chaotic situation that Father arrived, knowing full well that only two years previously another two missionaries had been murdered in the very province where he was to work. But he also knew that the only revolution which could save China was a revolution of the heart, leading men and women to follow Jesus Christ as their Lord and Saviour, and bring in the righteousness and justice of God as the new standards for the nation.

Within a year of Father's arrival Dr. Carr was forced to retire because of ill-health, and Father inherited the huge responsibility of being the only western-trained doctor and surgeon among the five million people of southern Shansi. The annual reports which he wrote of his twenty-two years there make fascinating reading. At times he had other doctors with him, and always one or two western nurses. They carefully trained local Christians to work as dispensers and assistant nurses. Despite exceedingly primitive equipment and a shortage of medicines, many people's sufferings were eased and diseases cured.

Early medical challenges

It is difficult to realize how limited medical knowledge was in those days. In 1916 an outbreak of bubonic plague swept down from the north and all doctors were ordered by the government to go and combat it. 'How did you fight it?' I remember asking Father. 'Did you have medicines?'

'No. There was no cure,' he replied. 'We just had to try and contain it by isolating the patients and burying the corpses. When our inspection teams arrived in town after town the mandarins [public officials] would insist they were quite clean. 'No, there is no plague here!' But we would walk down the road and find corpses lying in the street. I always had to lead the way when we were examining an area. We'd cover ourselves completely in long-sleeved overalls, boots and gloves, hoping the fleas that carried the plague couldn't bite us through our protection. The others were afraid unless I went in first. But the job of burying had to be done or the plague would have continued to spread.'

In those days they had nothing to reduce a high temperature, not even aspirin. Once on a medical trip into the mountains, both Father and his missionary nurse contracted typhus. She went down with it first and he followed twenty-four hours later. With a rapidly rising temperature, he had to arrange for two sedan-chairs to carry them back several days' journey to the hospital. It was their only hope of recovery. She quickly became delirious on the awful journey, jolted by the carriers, and died within a few days of reaching Linfen. Father ran an extremely high temperature. The only way they knew to get it down was to wrap him every fifteen minutes in a sheet wrung out in cold water. This treatment induced a state of shock. His burning skin would dry the sheet out and so cool him down a little. They told him later that his heart was pounding so loudly in the fight against the disease that it could be heard in the next room. Later he often wondered if it had been his long-distance running which had saved his life, as it developed strong heart muscles.

In their medical work they were up against deeply ingrained superstition and prejudice. Even after fourteen years in Linfen, Father wrote, 'In a courtyard not more than a stone's throw from our home we heard that they were still telling the children that the foreigners would dig out their eyes. Last year I was touring and a man came with a tumour, which I promised to remove . . . but he never came back. Later we heard the reason. He said to his friends, "If I let the foreigner take this off my leg, he will simply make it into medicine. And I do not enjoy being eaten by other people!" '

Father found a deep sense of satisfaction in the relief he was able to bring to many. I remember him describing removing cataracts for the elderly, an operation he could do fairly simply and quickly – and then the joy and amazement he saw on the patients' faces when they realized they could see again. A course in opthalmology had also trained him to prescribe glasses. Where these were obtainable the patient's vision could be improved even further.

But many cases were far more complicated. In 1928 he described 'a poor fellow who had received an injury to his jaw in childhood which prevented him opening his mouth even a quarter of an inch. Not only that, his teeth not having room to grow properly, had pushed each other out of shape. I attempted in vain to open his mouth. But what I could do was to make a hole for him. By means of pulling out teeth and removing bone, I made a round hole through which he could get quite a square meal.'

In the same report he describes 'another case which excited great comment . . . a man with an enormous tumour on the back of his neck, the size of my own head. Many Chinese doctors had refused to touch it. They told me after we had removed it what excitement there was in the city that the man was still alive after I'd removed it! . . . Another case was that of a poor child who would have come earlier but lived too far away. She had a growth behind the eye which pushed it out so far it was impossible for her to close the lids. She was always in tears with the pain and the disfigurement, feeling how strange it made her look. Her play-mates used to laugh at her. I'm glad to say I was able to remove the growth and make her look more normal again.'

Another report a few years later told how 'the daughter of our evangelist came here with a huge tumour. She could not have lived more than a few months. To operate was obviously so difficult and dangerous that at first I refused to attempt it. But the friends came to me and said, "We are all praying about this. We realize the danger, but we want you to operate. Even if she doesn't live, we would rather the attempt were made." I prayed about it for a day or two and there came to me the verse, "He that is perfect in knowledge is with thee." So, being strengthened, I operated, and all went well. She made an uneventful recovery and went home in three weeks.'

All this was done under conditions which were extremely primitive and difficult. For instance, water supply was always a problem. There were wells on the hospital compound, but the water from them was almost as bitter and unusable as sea-water. So water had to be carried in water-carts from a well half a mile away. This was very expensive and in dry weather there was barely enough. Only after sixteen or seventeen years was it possible to sink an artesian well, which eased the situation considerably.

Often they had to make their own medicine. An earlier missionary doctor had shown how crude sulphur, obtainable in China, could be boiled with lime, forming a liquid preparation which dealt very successfully with infections. Zinc oxide ointment could be made from the zinc lining of packing cases and the weak native spirit could be concentrated by distillation 'for use in tinctures and liniments'.

A missionary surgeon needed to be able to turn his hand to any medical need. So Father took a course in dentistry, and this became an additional facility which the hospital provided. One year he records checking and filling the teeth of forty missionaries and their children, as well as caring for local needs.

Robbers and Bandits

With the central Chinese government struggling to keep control and civil war frequently breaking out, banditry and robbery were common. The local people were often desperately poor and some joined the bands of brigands as the only way to get some food. Father often had to operate on soldiers who had gone into the mountains to fight against these roving bands. One such soldier had been wounded in the head and carried a piece of shrapnel embedded in his skull for three years before he turned up at the hospital. Father was able to locate and remove it (which was not easy without X-rays) and so earned the man's intense gratitude.

Another man said he had been attacked by robbers. Father reported, 'A bullet had entered the back of the neck and come out in front, smashing the jaw-bone. He was fortunate to escape with his life – a fraction to one side and the shot would have killed him. So we admitted him. But then the police came round and carried him off! It transpired that the man was a criminal, and had been captured and condemned to die. But the shot was misdirected. The man collapsed and his son carried him away for burial. On reaching home he discovered that his father still breathed. He placed him in the coffin and invited the relatives to the funeral. When night fell he got his father out, revived him, and filled the coffin with stones and padding, thoughtfully adding two pounds of pork. There was an elaborate funeral, and as it was July the pork produced the right atmosphere . . . but the police got wind of it! . . . I am convinced that but for an efficient police, the millions of people around us would be harried and tortured, have their houses burnt, their women carried off, and their old people and children held for ransom, just as is done in other provinces.'

From the report for 1933: 'A little boy of seven broke his arm. The fracture healed, but the elbow joint had grown together, so the arm was a rigid bar. The parents brought him 100 miles to us here. He was with us a month or more and went home with a movable joint. He spread the fame of the hospital. As a result another little boy came, this time with a large abdominal stone. When I handed it to his father, he gazed at it awestruck and exclaimed that our skill was like that of the gods!'

Bringing the message of Christ

The medical work was demanding, even sacrificial. But the main purpose of the hospital was to bring the love of Christ to the local people, and to show them the possibility of a richer and fuller life in fellowship with God. The very design of the buildings was planned to emphasize this. The large chapel, with its side-rooms for Sunday Schools and other meetings, stood in the centre, while the separate hospitals for men and women and the schools were grouped around it. As church members, the medical staff were all active in the church, as chairman, or a deacon or in some other way.

Within the hospital itself, the staff played a crucial part in evangelism. One or two Chinese evangelists were employed to talk with the out-patients while they waited to be seen, and to offer them gospels and tracts. Half an hour before surgery commenced a service would be held. Because this would often be the patients' only chance to hear the message, it was put over very simply and clearly. But those who were ill enough to be admitted as in-patients, together with the friend or relative who accompanied them, had a much better chance of understanding. Every afternoon a service was held for them. Later in the evening the hospital workers met for prayer and then scattered to the wards, carrying large gospel texts. They would teach the patients to read and to memorize them, while the evangelists would spend longer with any who showed greater interest. Also each member of staff was given particular responsibility for two or three patients. In these ways they tried to make the Christian message clear for all who came. The Chinese were fond of singing and the patients learnt many Christian hymns. Through-out the day, these could often be heard coming from the wards and reinforcing the message.

What was being presented was quite alien to the people of inland China. Steeped as they were in the idolatry and super-stition of folk religion, many disregarded it. But quite a number expressed interest and several came to faith. All these were followed up by passing on their names to the nearest church when they returned home, one to three days' journey away. The loving care and attention which they had received in the

Christian atmosphere of the hospital, away from the pressures of their own villages, began to bear fruit.

The Holy Spirit

The missionaries were very conscious that it was not their own efforts alone which would bring people to Christ. Father, grateful for the touch of the Holy Spirit on many patients' lives, wrote early on: 'This is spiritual work to be accompanied by spiritual weapons only. We beg you therefore that you would continually remember in prayer the medical work not only of Linfen but of all our CIM hospitals.'

In another article he emphasizes that 'our real need is indicated in the words of our Lord, "He that believeth on Me, out of his belly shall flow rivers of living water. This spake He of the Spirit which they that believe on Him should receive." It is these rivers of living water that people need.'

Many accounts of CIM missionaries at this time mention their dependence on the Holy Spirit's working and their longing for him to fill their lives. It is sometimes said that previous to the present generation the Holy Spirit was 'the forgotten person of the Trinity'. But this was far from true in missionary situations where they faced the stranglehold of idolatry and ignorance of Christ. The need for the Holy Spirit's working was much emphasized.

Social Concern

Father always showed a deep concern for the disadvantaged and under-privileged. He never saw the task of mission as being limited to 'saving souls', but cared about all the needs of the Chinese he met. Some modern mission thinkers seem to suggest that in previous generations evangelical missionaries focused on the spiritual aspect of mission without real concern for material and social needs. Reading Father's articles and knowing him so well myself, I can see that he strongly practised a holistic approach to mission. In researching this period I have found that such a concern for the whole person was common among many CIM missionaries.

He was painfully aware of the struggle for existence which dominated the lives of most of his patients and often referred to it in his articles. Famine frequently stalked the area; and he praised the energetic work of Shanxi province's Governor Yen, who did much to avert its worst consequences. His heart went out to the neighbouring province of Shenxi 'where ghastly conditions of brigandage and anarchy have prevailed for years; and now [June 1930] competent observers state that between one and two million people may die of starvation in the next few months.'

When refugees were pouring into a southern city some years later, and Father could be spared, he went to the assistance of Hayden Mellsop, the local CIM missionary, who was inundated with hundreds of needy folk. 'Driven from their homes and suffering untold hardship many pleaded [with the missionaries] for shelter and rest in Christian surroundings. With heart deeply moved, Hayden quoted: "The Master said, 'As you do it unto one of the least of these my brethren, you do it unto me.' " He continued, "The Lord who provided for Elijah knew our need, and from those funds administered by the CIM for refugees we have been able to care for these brothers and sisters in their hour of need. Of the 2,000 who have gone through our place here, 520 are still with us, and as we send these further west, others will fill up their places." ' In his report Hayden thanked Father, 'who three days a week came to inspect our camp and examine our sick.'

Medical Touring Teams

While he was working in Linfen Father had become concerned for the many patients who could not receive medical help because they found it difficult to reach the hospital. There were no tarmac roads, not even in the city. A man who was ill might stagger along the cart track, but a woman from an outlying village could not walk because of her tiny bound feet. In any case, women were not allowed to travel on their own, but must have their husband with them. To hire a sedan chair for thirty miles could cost a month's wages, which only the very rich could afford. So Father began to plan for a mobile clinic.

Both prayer and material preparation were needed. The team prayed much for the extra staff required and money for an additional set of operating instruments and a car. At the same time they trained skilled assistants who could give anaesthetics, sterilize instruments, do dressings and dispense medicines. But after some years all these aspects came together and they were able to meet the needs of a much wider area.

Father's missionary principles show clearly in his 1928 report. It would have been possible to use the mobile clinic for primary evangelism, going to villages where Christ had not been preached, but he and his colleagues held to their purpose of developing autonomous churches. So they let it be known they would take their touring team only if a church invited them for a planned medical mission. The church must take full responsibility, providing hospitality and their own teachers (both men and women) and making all the necessary arrangements.

One difficulty was to find a room in each village, where he could operate. Almost all the local houses were too small and dark and it was impossible to get good light. Then someone thought of the chapel. They all hesitated initially. Should a place appointed for worship be used for surgery? But recalling that our Lord did not hesitate to use a place of worship for his acts of mercy they went ahead and operated in the chapel in each town.

Father reported: 'We found this touring work a great help to the church. In every case the local leaders threw themselves into the work enthusiastically, arranging relays of preachers. From nine in the morning until six at night the courtyard of the church would commonly be crowded with people and continually there would be men and women proclaiming the good news of Jesus Christ to them. At Yicheng they had had special prayer for real conversions, and at one meeting two men stood up and announced that they intended to become believers.'

In this way Chinese Christians were encouraged to shoulder responsibility for Christian witness in their own area, while the missionaries were indicating: 'We are here to serve you, but not to take the lead.' When national churches are effectively evangelizing and teaching, missionaries may step more and more into the background. It was this kind of commitment to equipping the local church for grass-roots evangelism which meant that the church in China stood firm through all the later years of horrendous persecution from the Maoist government. Indeed they grew and multiplied, much to the amazement of some who thought Communism had obliterated Christianity.

The medical touring teams demonstrated another possibility for the future Chinese church. Father concluded his article with: 'Mission hospitals have been built by the generosity of friends in the west, but are far too elaborate for the native church to take responsibility for. . . . Why should not the Holy Spirit come upon some Chinese doctors and compel them to give up their lives for Christ? If so . . . it seems to me he might very well, and without charging at all too much, earn quite sufficient to support himself and his assistants by fees paid for operations and medicines, touring as we have done. At the same time he could actively preach the gospel.'

So Father was beginning to face the problem of institutional medicine, and to see that clinics in the community might be the answer. He could also foresee that there would be many professional Chinese Christians who would be prepared to sacrifice everything for the extension of Christ's kingdom.

Literacy Work

Another way in which the Christian community in Linfen attempted to meet local needs was by giving reading lessons. Chinese characters are notoriously difficult to master and most people who came to the hospital were illiterate. But the patients who stayed in the wards for some time had a good opportunity to begin to learn. The daily gospel teaching was given from two simple books, written as reading primers. They opened with sentences like:

'The Lord Jesus made the blind to see.
'The Lord Jesus made lepers clean.
'The Lord Jesus made the paralysed to walk.'

Although it took the whole day to master the first sentence, the patients discovered that learning to read was not impossible. Those who became Christians often showed the greatest motivation since they longed to be able to read the Bible for themselves.

The great Tianjin flood

The daily needs of the ordinary Chinese were enormous; but how much more desperate their situation became when catastrophes struck! In the late 1930s the city of Tianjin [Tientsin] and the surrounding countryside were struck by horrendous floods, causing extensive damage and huge loss of life. The word 'typhoon' comes from the Chinese tai-fung [big wind]. Two of these hurricanes, one closely following the other, struck further north than usual and deposited vast quantities of rain.

No one knew how many villagers drowned, but those who were able made their way to Tianjin which itself was under eight feet of water in places. The authorities threw open every available building, such as vacant warehouses and the grandstand of the racecourse. 1,600 refugees sheltered in the Tianjin Grammar School, filling every nook and cranny of the buildings. Other refugees crowded on to any high building or on to rooftops, clutching the few possessions they had been able to rescue. The Salvation Army at once got to work, co-operating with the authorities, and for two months organized a 'house-top' relief. Hiring boats, they went round from street to street distributing clean water and Chinese steamed bread and in this way helped some three thousand people daily. At the same time they called for medical assistance, because many of the destitute people were already weakened from three years of semi-famine, and disease spreads easily in such conditions. Father eagerly responded to their appeal.

As the waters slowly receded it was realized that the refugees could not return to their flooded plains before the winter set in. Some kind of shelter must be provided to shield them from the bitter cold. The city authorities allocated to the Salvation Army large stretches of waste land, where they erected hundreds of huts. The most economical way was to get the refugees to help. They dug long shallow trenches eight feet wide, then arched bamboo poles over them and covered these with stretched reed blinds to cover them. A space was left for a window and a door. The huts were plastered with mud to seal them from the biting winds. Sacking could be unrolled over the doors and windows when needed. The lines of huts were built facing due south so as to get the maximum warmth of the sun. The Salvation Army erected over 4,000 huts on various sites, caring for over 20,000 refugees.

I remember as a small child accompanying Father on one of his visits to these camps. The long low lines of huts stretched as far as I could see. Father had to stoop low to get through the door and could not stand upright inside. The Chinese family were pathetically grateful for his help. A little girl about my age stared at me, but we were both too shy to speak.

Reading Father's report on the great Tianjin flood, I see that the following spring the great plains had dried out, and the refugees could return. Thirteen thousand new suits of wadded clothes were distributed. Each family was given ten dollars and a bag of grain for sowing, and great barges carried them along the waterways to land as near as possible to their original homes. He concluded on a note of thankfulness: 'The whole enterprise was an amazing achievement. Thousands of poor peasants overtaken by a fearful catastrophe had been saved. Families had been kept together. They had been housed and fed for six months. Every able-bodied man had been set to work. Their illnesses had been cared for. Their children had been taught, and the Gospel had been preached to them.'

An indigenous church

Already, in Chapter One, we have referred to the question of indigenous self-propagating churches. Eighty years after Royal Wilder formulated his theories, Father also had strong convictions about this. In one of his annual reports he wrote:

'The thought that we are here to found a church is constantly before us in our work in the hospital. We aim not only to heal the sick but to set up a self-supporting, self-extending church that will be a permanent witness to Christ. And we are not vaguely slogging away, hoping that out of the converts a church will get itself formed some day, somehow. In co-operation with the rest of the Mission we aim to set up the church NOW.

'The church we wish to see in China must be truly indigenous, a natural growth of Chinese Christians, not a mere reproduction of some foreign form. It should be a church that meets all its own expenses, and is no more dependent on foreign money than our churches in England and America depend on subscriptions from China. It should be a church equipped with its own ministry: educated, spiritually-minded men and women, able to teach the

Christians what they should know, and to lead them in the practice of Christ's way of life. It should be a church which cares for the children, making such conditions in home and school that they are brought up in a Christian atmosphere, and that will be a spiritual home for men and women from the cradle to the grave. It should be a church that will carry the gospel throughout the whole of China and will send missionaries to the outlying provinces and Tibet.'

This report gives the lie to the idea that earlier missionaries were unaware of the need for truly indigenous church planting policies. Study of the mission practice of Father and his contemporaries reveals their clear goal for a genuinely Chinese church. Progressive steps were taken towards the fulfilment of this goal in spite of the predominant atmosphere of ignorance and superstition in inland rural China.

In 1929 Father was able to report on the visible progress which had been made. He described the work of a Chinese Christian, Dr. Li, who had been appointed two years previously when all foreigners had temporarily been forced to leave. 'Dr. Li led the church to such purpose that, after many years shivering on the brink, they took the plunge and decided that they would accept no more financial help from the Mission. . . . This is an event towards which we have worked for many years. . . . Other churches relinquished the annual subsidies gradually, but Linfen took the plunge suddenly. Having then to pay themselves for everything they did, they were brought down to essentials. All that they could do at first was to employ a caretaker.'

Father went on to explain that in China the first employee a church appointed was a chapel-keeper. He kept the guest room ready, welcomed early arrivals for services (they had no clocks to tell the time), answered enquiries and guarded the premises from robbers. When travelling, Christians could always stay in church guest rooms. So to be a Christian was to belong to a brotherhood that had homes everywhere.

After some years of employing a chapel-keeper the church in Linfen committed themselves to raising the salary for an evangelist as well. Later, when they felt they could afford it, they appointed a part-time pastor. All this necessitated the unprecedented step of taking up a weekly offering. At first the amount given was extremely small, but gradually it increased. The evangelist did an excellent job, spending practically all his time out in the villages. Carrying his own bedding, he walked from place to place, teaching and preaching, regardless of heat or cold. As Father remarked: 'Physical strength and willingness to rough it are essentials for a man who would shepherd the flock in Shansi.'

In 1934, after summarizing various steps forward, Father acknowledged, 'The church still has a long way to go before reaching true independence. The chapel with its guest room, classrooms and schools has been built but is still owned by the Mission, and the day for the actual transfer of the property is not yet in sight. The salary of the school teacher is provided by the Mission, and much of the work of the church is done by the hospital staff, whose salaries also come from abroad. But solid progress has been made, and I trust by the working of the Holy Spirit an indigenous church will one day be an accomplished fact.'

Over the years the number of Christians in Linfen district grew to about two hundred and they developed strong Christian leadership. Many of these were trained at the CIM Bible School in Hungtung, the nearest walled city. Sixty years after my parents left I had the joy of returning to Linfen. Any impression of a 'foreign religion' which the hospital and school might have given previously had long since been obliterated. The Christians had stood independent of any overseas assistance for many years.

Despite the fierce persecution of nearly fifty years of Communist rule, the church in Linfen today has grown to a thousand members. The leader is a fine eighty-year old woman who trained as a nurse under Father. We also met an elder who had become a Christian after receiving brain surgery from Father. It was very moving to sit in the church in Linfen and think back to what God had done over the years. We felt such a sense of joy and privilege as we talked and prayed together with the deeply spiritual Chinese Christians. The realization came afresh to me that Father's legacy lives on today.

As I think of Father's unwearying efforts in the hospital and his concern to widen the scope of the medical care by taking the hospital to the villages, I cannot help remembering those aunts in Reading. It is a long way from Reading to China, and feeding navvies is different from skilled surgery. But it is not fanciful to see the legacy here too – in the concern to care for people. As for the Brethrenism of his parents, the narrowness of which he rejected – Father's concern that each congregation should be self-supporting and answerable to Christ alone is very close to the original idea of the earliest Brethren. When Stanley Hoyte sailed for China he took with him his own family legacy and later left behind an enduring legacy for the Chinese Church.

Portrait of John Hoyte 1770–1846, Gamekeeper of the Duke of Rutland, Elizabeth's Great-great Grandfather on her Father's side.

Royal Gould Wilder and Eliza Jane Wilder, Elizabeth's Greatgrandparents on her Mother's side.

Henrietta Mary Hoyte and William Henry Hoyte, Elizabeth's Grandparents on her Father's side

Helene Valborg Wilder and Robert Parmalee Wilder, Elizabeth's Grandparents on her Mother's side.

The four Wilder sisters: Elizabeth, Grace, Ruth and Dorothy.

Grace Helene Hoyte and Dr Stanley
Hoyte, Elizabeth's parents.

Grace Hoyte with her six children: Robin, Eric, Rupert, Mary, John and
Elizabeth at Chefoo, N. China.

Grace Hoyte with Elizabeth as a baby.

Letter sent by Elizabeth from Japanese prison through the Red Cross.

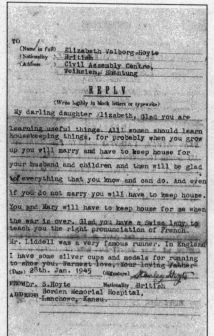

Her Father's reply on the back of Elizabeth's letter.

The Hoyte family a year after returning to England left to right:

| Eric | Mary | John | Rupert |
| Robin | Eileen | Stanley | Elizabeth |

Martin Goldsmith and Elizabeth Hoyte on their engagement day.

8-family houses in Lingga, the first village where the Goldsmiths helped in evangelism.

Evangelistic meeting inside an 8-family house.

Martin sharing the gospel with patients in Kabanjahe hospital.

Church women's group outside the Goldsmith's home in Kabanjahe.

Ruth Valerio, Elizabeth's youngest daughter, and her husband Greg.

Margaret Ellis, Elizabeth's eldest daughter, and her husband Roger.

Elizabeth and Martin with Ruth as a baby.

Chloe and James, Elizabeth's grandchildren, with their mother, Margaret.

Andrew Goldsmith, Elizabeth's son.

Elizabeth's family in 1998 left to right:
Roger   Greg
James   Margaret   Ruth   Chloe
Martin   Elizabeth   Andrew

Elizabeth with her childhood photo album.

Chapter 6

Her Price is Far above Rubies

Falling in love

The normal tour of service for CIM missionaries was seven years. But when Father first went to China he was young and single, and his skills as a doctor were badly needed, so he worked in China for almost ten years before returning home. As it happened, an American missionary who was seriously ill needed a medical escort home; Father was asked to return via America. Welcoming the opportunity to glean further medical knowledge at some of the leading American institutes, he also thought he would look up his old friend Robert Wilder, who by that time was back in the States with his family. He rang the doorbell and was greeted by Grace, grown from the slip of a teenager he remembered into a lovely young woman. He fell in love with her on the spot, extending his stay in that city so as to be able to visit her again and again.

Grace was of slender build, with long thick brown hair and twinkling eyes. She had a lively personality and was full of fun and shared his love of the out-doors. He was delighted to discover that she too was preparing for missionary work in China, the only one of the four Wilder daughters to follow the missionary calling of their parents.

Grace's upbringing had endowed her with a rich heritage. The many friends who came to her parents' home made her feel at ease with people of any nationality. From her parents too she had learned the joys of hospitality, noticing the needs of each guest and helping them to feel at home. The long summers in

Norway had given her a love of mountains and lakes and from her maiden aunt, Tante Aagot, she had learned to paint with water colours and oils. Weaving rugs in bright Norwegian designs was another of her skills and she loved to write in beautiful italic script with vividly ornamented capital letters. The Norwegian delight in the outdoors appeared in her zest for hiking and skiing, rowing and fishing. She could quickly build a campfire and was used to sleeping out under the stars. In later years when her children attended the CIM school at Chefoo [Yantai], it was she who initiated Scouts and Guides and taught the many skills involved. The teenagers loved the varied activities and thoroughly enjoyed the new challenges, so different from their academic work.

But that lay ahead. To Father's bitter disappointment, Grace said 'No' to his marriage proposal, and he had to return to England alone. But soon afterwards, intending to study in England before sailing for China, she wrote asking if he could meet her and take her to Livingstone College in North London where many new missionaries went to gain some medical knowledge. Here the courtship continued. Finally her heart was won, and they were bowled over with joy as they began to know each other more deeply. But CIM rules in those days were that marriage must be delayed until certain language exams were passed. Father made the unusual suggestion that Grace should study Chinese at the School of Oriental and African Studies in London instead of waiting to begin in China. He was never one to toe the orthodox line and it's natural to suppose that he felt some impatience at having to sail back to China without her!

In July 1924 they were married in Shanghai. He was nearly forty and she was only twenty-seven. But they were deeply in love and spent nearly twenty happy years together. Father often said she mastered the Chinese language better than he did. In view of his busy medical schedule this was not surprising. She had a great gift for evangelism and gave herself to the female staff of the hospital and the women patients, endearing herself to every one. People have told me that she never lost the enthusiasm of youth. Warm-hearted, very informal and at times a trifle chaotic, she always bubbled over with life.

Mother had longed for six children and that was what God gave her – in just over nine years! We must have been a handful! But our parents made a wonderful home for us. And we never felt we lacked for anything, even though life was so primitive in China in those days.

After some years they were able to buy an old Chinese mill in a pretty valley with a little millstream running through. The money came as a legacy from William Henry Hoyte, who had become a successful architect/builder. He left a double portion to each of his three missionary children, realizing the sacrifice they had made. Mother and Father found great joy in renovating the mill and damming the stream to form a pool for us children to swim in. They turned a little turret into a quiet prayer room with extensive views across the rural countryside. We came to the mill each August to escape the heat of the hottest month, and relax and enjoy times together as a family. Many missionary friends also made use of the mill for a holiday – among them Leslie Lyall, who later became a prolific writer on China, and who courted his Kathy while staying there. I wonder if the mill was Mother's idea, reminding her of how the family used to retreat to Norway for rest and refreshment when she was a girl.

Besieged by the Communist Army

But times were difficult in China during the 1930s. General Chiang Kai-Shek, leader of the Nationalist Party, was struggling to gain control of the whole country. Mao Zedong and his Communist followers were determined not to surrender. Driven out of their strongholds in the south in 1934, Mao and his troops set out on an epic journey of six thousand miles which came to be known as 'the Long March'. Crossing high mountains and hazardous rivers, they worked their way in a wide arc right across the western areas of China, then sweeping north they finally found shelter in the loess caves across the great Yellow River from Shansi. As they journeyed they left a trail of death and destruction, often slaughtering the landlords and wealthier farmers and stealing their goods at will. The helpless people lived in terror of the Red Army and no one's life was immune from danger.

In December 1934 the Communists murdered two young American CIM missionaries, John and Betty Stam. Their three-month-old baby Helen was saved only because a Chinese Christian offered his life for hers. The Red Army also captured Alfred Bosshardt, a Swiss CIM missionary, and forced him to march for 2,500 miles with them in terrible conditions. Arnolis Hayman was his fellow prisoner for over a year.

1934 was the year when I was born in Linfen, the youngest of six children. My three older brothers were away at school and I was barely walking when the ominous news arrived that some sections of the Red Army had crossed the Yellow River and were pillaging our province. Like other larger towns, Linfen was surrounded by magnificent high walls, ten feet across, and furnished with strong gates. The Mandarin assured the missionaries that they were protected by five hundred soldiers and so would be safe from attack. But rumours began to fly around, some of them all too true. I have a precious document, written on an old typewriter, and entitled, 'We are Besieged', in which Mother described, with reticence and courage, what then transpired.

The first indication that the Communists were coming was the news that the railway to the north had been cut and with it all access to the provincial capital. Then the hospital steward returned from the station to announce that all the railway officials had boarded the last train and were gone. The five hundred soldiers who were supposed to protect the city had fled south and panic was spreading. The Mandarin had given orders for the city gates to be closed. There was no way they could escape now, and yet only a few local militia remained to protect them. 'At each piece of news our hearts sank a little lower', she wrote. Father attempted to send a wire to Shanghai, while the other missionaries 'knelt down and laid the matter before the Lord.' She continues:

> 'Was I afraid? I was not afraid of actually dying at their hands. But I was afraid for the children. I should have liked to protect them from being scared or hurt. And yet as I faced this fear, I knew that if I set the right standard, they would be as brave as I wanted them to be. Children are heroes at heart, for all heroic stories appeal greatly to them. So I trusted God to give me courage and strength when the time came to show them how to be brave . . .
>
> Then came another question. What if we were killed and the children left? I had a talk with good old Mrs. Teng, our children's nurse, who said of course she would do her best for them in that case. And let me say here, what a help it is in such straits to face each question honestly and to talk them out with the person concerned. It is wonderful what strength God gives for it.
>
> Then came another question. What about our three boys at school? We faced it together. It would seem terrible to deprive them of a mother's and father's loving sympathy and continual care. And yet as Stan said, "God has done wonderful things through orphans." It was a great relief to write Robin a long letter, telling him of the facts and of what might happen to us, saying how brave we knew he and his brothers would have been if here, and urging them to keep close to Jesus all their lives. I wonder if the letter ever reached him. Perhaps the Reds got it instead. Then we asked God to enlighten our minds to show us what we should do in order to "Be prepared" '.

The next day word came that the missionaries in a nearby town had left for Kaifeng.

> 'We hear that the last train which left yesterday full of railway officials got to a place twenty miles away when they met with

bandits. So they all came back again! We are glad to have them back.

'We were assured today that soldiers from the south had arrived at the station, one mile outside the city, and were firing at the Red Army whom they saw at a distance. This made us very hopeful. But this evening we were told that it was not the soldiers, but the Reds, who had taken possession of the station and were firing at the city!'

So rumours swung back and forth.

Spies were sent out over the walls of the city to find out what they could. Many were beaten and killed, but a hunchback and a boy managed to return. The crackling of gunfire could often be heard, interspersed with the booming of the four cannon which the city owned. Mother describes how my big sister Mary, aged five, stood in the garden and counted the booms.

A few days later the Communists attacked Hungtung. This was the nearest walled city to Linfen. The CIM had built a Bible School there where many local church workers were trained. The boys from the D.E. Hoste school just outside Hungtung only just managed to escape before their buildings were over-run. The city contained many Chinese Christians as well as seventeen missionaries and their children. With few soldiers to guard them, it was only God's protecting hand which prevented the Communists from entering. Ammunition was scarce, so lime was hurled in the faces of the attackers. I have a photo showing the walls of the city streaked with white after this episode.

If the Red Army captured a city they would usually stay four or five days, looting all the buildings, dragging the richer landowners off for mock trials, and killing whom they pleased. Often they would then move on. So Father and Mother hit on the plan of making a hiding place. When and if the Communists came to Linfen, we could all be hidden and might survive the city's capture.

Mother's report contains two cryptic sentences: 'Stan is feeling responsible for all the hospital staff. He has got two fine places of escape for the hospital.' What these were I will never know. Their secret place for us as a family was made by bricking up a doorway which led into two old storerooms in the corner of the courtyard. As she wrote, the only way of reaching them would then be by scrambling onto the kitchen roof, over a small sloping roof, and across the great main roof which was large and sloped quite sharply, so much so that a man might well hesitate to walk on it. At the other end a ladder would be standing, down which we could climb. Father and Mother furnished these two rooms with a bed, some mattresses, boxes for storing bedding and food, a stove and a chimney, a chair and stools, washbasin, pails, a candle and matches, and paper and pencils for the children. They also put in a store of coal, kindling and paper and a water-butt, while a local bricklayer blocked off the entrance. They were a bit anxious about him as he was a talkative old man. Mother commented: 'It is impossible to do anything secretly in this country. . . . The bricklayer thinks we want to put our treasures there. And so we do, for our children are our treasures.'

She continued: 'Mary is perfectly sweet about it all. She is the only child who can understand. Having heard all about Peter Pan and the pirates, it seems to her as if she were living in an exciting book. She skips along over the roof, climbs boldly down the ladder, and helps me put away all sorts of useful things.' I have been told that Mother and Father practised climbing over the roof with John aged three and me as a baby in their arms.

More days dragged by with wild rumours circulating. Each shop in the city had to provide men to do guard duty at night and a bright lantern which could be hung over the side of the walls to foil a surprise attack. Occasionally bombing could be heard in the distance and sometimes aeroplanes were seen flying overhead. That might be one way of escaping. They sent a telegram to ask if a plane could land and take them off.

One day a packet was dropped with instructions to prepare a landing strip for a plane, and hopes began to soar. Mother set to work packing boxes. Father busied himself making arrangements for the hospital staff. If we were able to get away the Mission would not be able to pay their wages and Father wanted to make sure they had enough food in case there was a long siege. But day after day passed and no plane arrived. Later they learned that the landing strip was not long enough. Subsequently they asked for an autogiro (as a helicopter was called in those days) but none came. There was only one helicopter in North China.

Mother taught her Sunday School class as usual: 'It was strange to sit there facing these little Chinese girls, looking at their bright smiles in response to mine, and wondering if we should soon meet in Heaven. Of course one has always in the background of one's mind the thought that we may be called upon to give up our lives. My heart is at rest. . . . God knows all about it, and it is lovely to trust the outcome to Him.'

Relief finally came nearly a week later when the British Consul, Lovat Fraser, arrived in the provincial capital and sent word that he would reach them in a few days' time. So our secret hiding place was never actually needed. But as I grew up I could sense the calibre of my parents through this account of how they faced danger, and were kept in peace through their trust in God.

Family life in Chefoo

In 1937 Mother and Father went on furlough for the second time. The earlier furlough had been in 1927, when all expatriates had been forced to leave because of further anti-foreign riots. After this second furlough Father worked for a while in Kaifeng, capital of Honan. Then he was posted to the Chefoo missionary boarding schools where my four older brothers and my sister were already studying.

Father and Mother had found it hard to send the older children off to boarding school. But now we had a wonderful year while Father worked as the school doctor, and we could all be together as a family. Looking back, I can see God gave us this special time in readiness for what was to come.

The Chefoo schools were situated right by the sea in the healthy climate of northern Shantung [Shandong] Province. Here as a family we swam and dived, rowed out to sea or picnicked on other beaches further away. There were rolling hills behind the town to explore, and temples and monasteries to visit. Each winter when thick snow covered the ground we went tobogganing. One year it was so cold the sea froze across the wide bay. Mother and Father encouraged us to bring friends home after school; the parents of these other children were far away serving the Lord in other parts of China.

We developed family traditions too. Mother managed to give each of the six of us individual attention. We each had our 'importance day' when it was our turn to have fun with her in the kitchen and turn out a surprise for the rest of the family. This made learning to cook a special treat. On Saturdays she took one of us in turn downtown to do the weekend shopping. We had the delight of choosing eight special cakes from the bakery to eat as a Sunday treat. We benefited from the Olsson way of life, and as Mother had always looked forward to Sundays as a child she made our Sundays special. We went to church together, and then played a game walking home while Father quizzed us to see if we had understood the service.

There would often be an outing to some interesting place after the delicious Sunday dinner. Then in the evening Father would read aloud from *Swallows and Amazons* or *Black Beauty* with his rich, expressive voice. The day would finish by listening to music, as our parents had brought one of the early gramophones back to China with them. As a six-year-old I remember the privilege of being allowed to turn the heavy handle to wind it up. But only the older ones were allowed to change the thick needle and

carefully swing the head over to rest on the swirling black disk.
So Mendelssohn's Violin Concerto or Beethoven's Kreutzer
Sonata floated out on the evening air.

Of course there were family disagreements too. I was round
and tubby, and being the smallest became the easy target for
frequent teasing, especially from one of my brothers. But we
need to learn to cope with life's difficulties as well as its joys.

Father passed on to us children his fascination with science.
The school asked him to give some lectures on the human body
and he held staff and children spell-bound as he described the
delicate mechanism of the eye or how the muscles of the arm
contract. He was intrigued with mystery of every kind and would
go out of his way to investigate it. Returning to England via
Egypt one furlough, he sought to find out how and why the
pyramids were built. A visit to Stonehenge left him fascinated
with how it was constructed and what was its meaning. Long
before most people had even heard of it, Father travelled to Turin
to see the Shroud and make a careful medical assessment of it. I
believe my own love of science began in those early days when
I was just starting at school.

Our biggest treat as a family came that summer when we
went camping on Lighthouse Island, five miles out to sea. John,
my youngest brother, and I were allowed to come only if we
could swim right round the raft which was anchored opposite
the school. I remember the elation of puffing and panting as I
finally made it round by doggy-paddle. Mother organized
enough food for two weeks, and Father sorted out the tents,
camp beds, charcoal stoves etc. Then a hired launch deposited
us, our camping gear and a row boat onto a shingly beach. For
two glorious weeks we explored rock pools, rowed out to
distant outcrops, laughed and played, swam and sketched, and
listened to our beloved gramophone under the starlight. Then
a huge thunderstorm broke and we had to take shelter with the
lighthouse keeper. But nothing could mar the joy of that
holiday.

With six children at the school, Mother and Father asked the Mission leaders if they might remain at Chefoo. But a crisis had developed in the hospital at distant Lanchow [Lanzhou], capital of the north-western province of Gansu, and Father's help was needed there. Mother hated to show us children how much she felt the parting. She did not want to add to our distress, but spoke brightly of the holidays we would have together. Yet as she left me, her youngest, she completely broke down in the headmistress's room after I had left. It took great courage to compose herself and face the future. Fortunately for us all, we did not know then that she would never see us again.

Journey across No Man's Land

It was now 1940 and the Japanese had been forcibly gaining control over large areas of China. Father and Mother faced a hazardous journey of over a thousand miles, which would take them across the fighting zone. There were long delays and much danger in crossing the front lines. The first part of the journey took at least a week, travelling by ship to Tianjin [Tientsin], and then on to Beijing for their military passes. After that they could catch a train for part of the way, but then the railway line ended. So all their cases of personal belongings, medical equipment and supplies for the interior had to be hoisted on to handcarts and securely tied down.

What made the journey ten times more difficult was the huge floods they had to negotiate. In order to impede the Japanese advance, the Chinese army had breached the dikes of the Yellow River, allowing it to flood hundreds of square miles of the wide plains of Honan province. Thousands of villages were swamped and the roads obliterated, leaving vast uncharted lakes. Four times Father and Mother and their two missionary friends had to cross the waters, each time hiring boatmen who often did not know the way themselves.

The first flooded area was over twenty miles wide. After a great deal of haggling a price was fixed and the handcarts began to be unloaded into six big flat-bottomed punts. The trunks and heavy boxes were placed at the bottom, the other goods stowed into nooks and crannies, and the handcarts balanced on top. The travellers squeezed themselves into whatever space they could find and the boatmen heaved the boats forward using long punting poles. Sometimes they paddled with crude oars made of a piece of rough wood tied to a pole. Two of them scraped at the water with spades!

Progress proved extremely slow and the boatmen found few landmarks to guide them. Overhanging branches threatened to catch the top-heavy boats and overturn them. Sometimes they appeared to be following the track of an old road. At other times they missed the way and wandered across fields. Night fell and they were still far from the other side. Meandering through misty moonlight, but with unfailing optimism, the boatmen pushed and pulled, and finally at about 10 p.m. tied up at a village they knew. Here was a narrow strip of land six feet wide and crowded with people: soldiers, food-sellers and villagers. Tying their boats to some trees, their boatmen disappeared to eat, while the missionaries looked for somewhere to unroll their bedding for the night.

But it was not to be. Word soon came that robbers were around. So they hurriedly set off once more.

This time they hired a pilot who claimed to know the way. About midnight the moon went down. The clouds scattered and the stars came out with a brilliance which Father had seldom seen before. But about 3 a.m. the pilot announced in a melancholy voice that he was lost! 'How can you be lost when you can see the stars?' the others demanded. But lost as they were, there was no alternative but to press on. After another hour they found themselves in a good stream which carried them along at a better pace, when – crash! There was a terrific bump. The boat was jerked to a halt and the boatman in front was hurled head first into the water. They had hit a submerged stump, and the inrush of water could be heard. Everyone sprang into action.

Fortunately they were not far from a hut which had collapsed into a pile of mud covered with the wet straw of its roof. Hastily the punt was unloaded. Carts, trunks, boxes, bedding, backpacks, food basket, gramophone, typewriter and their unfortunate owners were dumped unceremoniously onto the mud pile. It seemed a long wait until dawn broke, and even longer before another boat could be hired. This one was half the size and even more unsteady than the previous one. But eventually they set off across the swirling waters, and some hours later reached the other side.

Travelling across dry land proved not much better. The bumpy roads were mere rough tracks. The Chinese men hauling the handcarts walked very slowly. Father and one of the other missionaries rode bicycles, and would cycle ahead and then wait by the roadside reading a book. Incongruous as it may seem, Father was enjoying the life of the poet Shelley and a biography of General Smuts. Mother brought up the rear, making herself responsible for all the baggage. They bought what food they could find along the way. Father commented that the inns were the worst he had ever seen. The rooms had mud walls and thatched roofs, no doors and not even paper in the windows. They usually preferred to sleep on threshing floors out under the stars. Father observed the country folk in the villages they passed:

> 'It was a depressing sight, open mouths, wrinkled foreheads, dull, blank, staring eyes in which no gleam of intelligence seemed to shine. But these are people for whom Christ died, and it is out of just such ordinary folk that most of the present Christian Church has been formed. And when the Gospel has entered in, what a difference it makes! One can often tell from a person's face that he is a Christian. Christians commonly look brighter, more vigorous, more pleasant. We came into touch with a number on the journey.'

In this difficult and painfully slow manner they pressed on, negotiating further stretches of flood water and bumpy terrain. At one point they fell into the hands of a brigand chief. His face was hard and cruel and he flaunted a large pistol; his aggressive manner appeared very threatening. However, Father was able to treat his cook's ulcerated leg, and eventually they were allowed to continue. They were fired on as they crossed the wide river from Japanese controlled territory into free China. Then they narrowly escaped imprisonment for heroin smuggling when someone hid forty-eight packets of the incriminating drug in their baggage. But God brought them safely through.

To their dismay, the Nationalist army then informed them that they had crossed the Yellow River at the one place where it was forbidden. Consequently they were held under house arrest for several weeks. But good came out of even this delay. Father took time to write a detailed account of this part of the journey and called it 'Across No-man's Land'. Mother illustrated it with beautiful pen and ink sketches down the margins and across the pages. I still have this precious document. There are drawings of the floods, their flat-bottomed punts, villages which they passed, little girls with sticking-out pigtails and many delightful scenes. The last words are:

> 'The weather is getting colder. We have high mountains to cross before we reach Lanchow. And it will be bitterly cold on the way. However our times are in God's hands, and we expect to get off before too long.'

As I retell the story, I realize that part of what my parents passed on to me was this steady determination to obey God no matter what difficulties presented themselves, coupled with a quiet confidence in God's sovereign care. It stood me in good stead when I had to put God's faithfulness to the test in a Japanese prison camp. With this in mind, I later called my life-story *God can be Trusted*. I too proved that I could put my life entirely in God's safe hands. He would always be with me; and all that would happen to me could be only within his purposes of love.

Arrival in Lanchow

I have no idea how long it took Father and Mother to reach far-off Lanchow. Years later, after a railway was built, my husband and I were able to travel there. From Xi'an, the ancient Chinese capital now famous for its terracotta army, our train took twenty-nine hours. Looking out of the window, watching the miles trundle by, I noticed a cart-track running parallel to us much of the way, possibly the very road along which Mother and Father had travelled. I tried to visualize them making their slow progress day after day. What would Mother have been feeling as the distance grew ever greater between her and her children? Surely she must have realized then that it would be quite impossible for us to visit them during our annual school holidays.

It *was* impossible. We never came home to Father and Mother. The Japanese hold on the north grew tighter and tighter. Then came December 1941 and Pearl Harbour; and suddenly we foreigners were no longer neutrals in a Sino-Japanese war. We too were now caught up in the war. Mother and Father heard the news that the Japanese army had imprisoned us in Chefoo school. Some months later our buildings were requisitioned, and the whole school was crammed into a few houses on the other side of town. The following year they heard that we had all been moved to a prison along with some 1,400 other aliens from the Beijing and Shantung [Shandong] areas. Letters became fewer and fewer.[1]

---

[1] I have written in more detail about these years in a prison camp in *God can be Trusted*.

Meanwhile Father had taken up the leadership of the CIM hospital in Lanchow. This had been built in 1913 with money left by William Borden of Yale, whose longing had been to win Muslims for Christ. There were many Chinese Muslims in that area and Gansu formed the gateway to Xinjiang, where many other Muslim peoples lived. Dr. Rupert Clarke, who was junior to my parents, many years later wrote to my sister Mary describing the situation at the Borden Memorial Hospital when my parents arrived:

'The coming of your Father and Mother to Lanchow was a great help to us, as the sort of 'democratic unity' form of running the hospital had broken down completely, and the hospital was creaking along very poorly. Stan had been told by International Headquarters to run the place on his own. He was sufficiently senior to us all to be able to do it without any real friction. As you know he was a very wise and gracious man. . . .

'Your Mother was a very enthusiastic person – enthusiastic for the Lord, and a diligent evangelist . . . Previous to coming to Lanchow she had been largely concerned with the bringing up of her family. But being unwillingly freed from that responsibility she threw herself into evangelism with great zeal . . . The elder's wife remarked that she was *je-xin-hu-tu* (chaotically enthusiastic). But the elder's wife had come from a very staid Presbyterian background. And there is a great need for a few people who are *je-xin-hu-tu* to counteract formality. I think she would have been a good charismatic these days.'

I was interested to read Rupert Clarke's description as I also react to undue formality in the Christian church.

Mother or Father wrote to each of the six of us practically every week until we were imprisoned. Then they had to wait for Red Cross forms to arrive on one side of which we had written, leaving the back empty for their reply. I have a store of treasured letters from them, each of mine written in clear script as I was aged seven or eight and had not yet learned 'long-hand'. With loving care

Mother took time to do a little sketch in the corner: a tiny daisy as I was her smallest, a white narcissus against a blue background when the wild ones were bursting into flower, forget-me-nots or a sprig of cherry blossom, or a fairy combing her hair. I have often thought that my love of nature and of beauty sprang from these delicate illustrations. Their letters were full of love and courage, urging me to be good and helpful. From time to time comes a sentence like, 'It is three years since we saw you and we are longing to see you again. There are crowds of children playing in the garden outside. They have come to Sunday School, and we like to have them come and play here first.'

Knowing Mother's gift with children, her longing to see us must have been very great. One of the lady missionaries told me years later that she would sometimes find Mother with tears in her eyes. But she never allowed her heartache to hinder her work for the Lord, and she made a lovely home for Father to return to after the stresses of hospital life.

The hospital was situated across the river from the main city, on the north bank where the air was cleaner and where it could catch the most direct sunlight. Unfortunately nobody had realized that the local Muslims believed that an ill person must not be carried over water. Because this made it difficult for them to come to the hospital a clinic was held daily on the church premises in the city. Crossing the river came to have a special significance for Mother. A great iron bridge had been built over the Yellow River at Lanchow by some Belgian engineers when oil was discovered further into the interior. Every time Mother went to take a meeting or do some shopping she would have to cross this iron bridge; and she would always spend the time praying for each of her children.

Over fifty years later it was very moving for us to walk the length of the bridge ourselves, thanking God for her dedication, and placing once more into his arms of love all her heartache and sacrifice.

Family Tragedy

It was at the height of the fighting, when Lanchow was being bombed by Japanese planes, and Father was up to his eyes caring for the wounded, that the unthinkable happened.

The story is told in one of Father's letters which I treasure most deeply. Written to his sister, it is dated 21 December 1943.

My dearest Fraie,

You will have received my wire [telegram]. My darling wife is gone. I am still broken by the shock. We had thought and planned so much for the wonderful future – when we should have the children once more. But we never seriously thought of THIS.

It came very suddenly and swiftly. She had not been altogether well for a couple of months . . . carrying a heavy burden of work. I kept her in bed most of Monday. She got up in the evening to attend a meeting, but felt cold and sick. By Friday her temperature was 103. I got her to bed with a fire, for it is bitterly cold now. Her temperature went up higher, and by Monday she was wandering. Then each day marked a day of further prostration. She spoke with more and more difficulty; and then the rash came out and we knew it was typhus. I had thought it might be relapsing fever so had tried sulphonamides, but it had no effect. The temperature stayed between 104 and 105 for five or six days, and the pulse over 140.

'As soon as we knew she was seriously ill, Dr. Rupert Clarke and Jeanette who is a trained nurse moved over here to live with me. They took charge of the nursing, and relieved me of medical work and advised as to treatment. So she had the best of care. I looked after her all night, and the others took over in the day. I am glad I was with her so much. I had a terrible fear that it was the last thing I should ever be allowed to do for her. It was dreadful to see her lying there, burnt up with fever . . . The last night I gave her saline under the skin, dripping it in a drop at a time. [Saline was not at that time given intravenously.]

Then the temperature began to fall, and at half-past two she began to perspire. That is just what I did when I had it 22 years ago, and I was so glad. And here I thanked God. This was the crisis I expected, now the fever was disappearing and in a few hours she would be over it – very weak but over the danger. I kept her warm with blankets and warmed the room, neither too hot nor too cool. But in the morning she changed colour and collapsed. I called for help. We did all we could, wrapped her in a warm blanket, injected adrenalin and cardiazole in a desperate attempt to save her. But it was no good.

O dear, O dear! I wish you were here or some of the children. It's terribly lonely. We've been desperately in love for 20 years and now she is gone. . . . I can face most things in life with a certain amount of firmness, but whenever Grace is in danger I lose my nerve. I don't think I have loved her too much, but I do think I have been too absorbed in her. . . . I seemed alone until when I was nearly 40 I found Grace and gave myself away completely. . . .

It takes a great effort to be cheerful and hopeful. One has to fix one's mind steadily on other people and their needs, and determine to forget oneself. But that is the right thing, and truly following Christ means making the effort.

With warm love to you all
Your loving brother,
Stan

Poor Father! How lonely he must have felt without Mother and with his children so far away. Rupert and Jeanette Clarke were very loving and stayed in his home to keep him company. But of course it was not the same. He told me years later that there are times in life when all one can do is just cling on. You may feel terrible and the situation may be awful. But keep holding on, doing what is right for each day; and trusting that one day God will bring the dreadful darkness to an end.

Father had a headstone cut for Mother's grave with the simple inscription based on Proverbs 31:10.

IN LOVING MEMORY OF GRACE HELENA HOYTE . . .
HER PRICE IS FAR ABOVE RUBIES.

On our visit to Lanchow my husband Martin and I tried to find her grave. We showed a photo of it to the hospital authorities. Chinese respect for the dead ensured that they were very understanding; but all trace of it was gone. However, they took us to a small patch of land at the far end of the hospital complex overlooking the river, which they felt might have been the place. Three small peach trees had been planted there, looking fragile and bare in the hazy February sunshine. But as I looked at them I knew that although they looked so dead, actually they were alive. In the spring they would burst into beautiful blossom. So too Mother is not dead, but shines with a resurrection beauty beyond anything she knew on earth.

Joy in spite of suffering

Martin and I went across to the city to find the church where Mother and Father had worshipped. Again what a joy it was to meet some of the present leadership; fine Chinese Christians, dedicated to making Christ known. An elderly evangelist remembered Father and Mother clearly. In fact he missed being in the photo of Father's farewell, which I brought with me, only because he had been out in the villages preaching the gospel. We went into the church, a large building with a big gallery on three sides, which could easily hold 1,000 people. They told us that the previous Christmas they filled it three times over with 3,000 people at each service! And now they were planning to build a much larger church. What dynamic

Christians they were! We knew that through the Communist years they had been willing to endure much suffering for their faith. My eyes brimmed with tears of joy as I began to realize something of the extent of the harvest of the past missionaries' labours.

Then they took us to another entrance and announced with great joy, 'We feel safe at last to expose it!' There on the floor lay a pile of plaster which had been covering, and so protecting, the foundation stone of the church. Through the powdery surface we could clearly see the words

CHINA INLAND MISSION

1923

TO THE GLORY OF GOD

One of them remarked, 'It was only the missionaries of the China Inland Mission who were prepared to travel such a long way, and live in such remote areas with all its hardships, to bring us the gospel. They set us a model of suffering, and we have followed their example.' As we looked into their faces we felt humbled at all that they had been through and yet deeply thankful that God had preserved and blessed them, watering the seed which Mother and Father had sown.

As for Father, during the last year of the war he received no letter from the six of us. So he had no proof that we were still alive. I have described in *God can be Trusted* how, when the war was over, he at last obtained permission to leave Lanchow, made his way across the chaotic, war-torn countryside, with pot-holed roads and broken bridges, and finally managed to meet up with us in Hongkong in October 1945.

I was both excited and apprehensive when someone called to me, 'Elizabeth, your Father has come!' Would I recognize him? What was he like? How would it feel to be together after five years? But I need not have feared. His big strong arms were soon around me. And so began the gentle, probing process of getting to know each other again.

BIBLIOGRAPHY
for Chapters 5 and 6

Coad, F. Roy, *A History of the Brethren Movement* (Exeter: Paternoster, 1968)

Broomhall, A.J., *Hudson Taylor and China's Open Century* (London: Hodder and Stoughton, 1982)

Broomhall, Marshall, The Jubilee Story of the China Inland Mission (Morgan and Scott, 1915)

Lyall, Leslie T., *A Passion for the Impossible* (Hodder and Stoughton, 1965)

Taylor, Mrs. Howard, *The Triumph of John and Betty Stam* (China Inland Mission, 1936)

Watson, Jean, *Bosshardt: A Biography* (OMF International, 1995)

Also

Various articles from *China's Millions* written by Dr. Stanley Hoyte

Other unpublished papers

Chapter 7

The Baton Passes On

The baton of the family heritage was now being passed on to me, although I was too young to realize it at the time. Having been separated from my parents for five years, now at the age of eleven I barely knew anything of the legacy that was mine. And yet as our family returned to England and tentatively put down roots in what for us was a strange environment, I began to catch glimpses of the inheritance which surrounded me.

A strong confidence in a God who loved us and cared for us formed the foundation. The seven of us arrived penniless – no home, no mother, no job for Father, and with very few possessions. Yet the wider family of uncles and aunts opened their homes to us. We were given places in schools and colleges. Eventually Father found a job with a house large enough for us all to live together at last. At the age of sixty this was for him in itself a miracle of God. And – the biggest step of all – he married Eileen Drake, a woman brave enough to take on the task of being mother to six adolescents straight out of a Japanese prison.

I had the privilege of being born into a close-knit family, where each one of us was loved and appreciated. In days when sexism ruled, we girls were treated equally with the boys. 'Male and female, both in the image of God' was Father's strong belief. We were all alike encouraged to work hard and blossom, reaching our potential no matter in what direction that lay. We were also given a strongly biblical foundation for our lives. While still young, we had been told Bible stories. As we grew older we were encouraged to read the Word of God for ourselves, so as to grow to know it intimately. Our missionary teachers in China helped us to learn by heart many psalms and other passages from the Bible. What is memorized in youth often remains deeply embedded, so that I can still recall some of these passages of Scripture. In these ways I learned early in life that to follow scriptural principles was the only way to true happiness and fulfilment.

The heritage was there. After having been cut off from it by our years of deprivation and isolation, how would each of us handle the life which lay before us? We all felt bewildered by the traumatic events we had lived through. Our close-knit family had been wrenched apart. Above all, the one who should have been at the centre, drawing us all together, had been snatched from us.

Perhaps it was hardest for those who were older. Rob, my much loved oldest brother, suffered a tragic breakdown and never fully recovered. Another brother felt angry over the treatment he had received as a growing teenager from the missionary staff of the school who had themselves felt the burden of responsibility, caring for other people's children, and so had been unduly strict and inflexible. My sister had reacted strongly to the news of Mother's death. 'She was the person I loved above everyone else. . . . With Mother gone, what's the point of being good?' She began to earn a reputation as a rebel. But all the time a deep chasm of loneliness ached inside her.

My unconscious reaction was to withdraw into an emotional shell. As it hardened, it would protect me from all the bewildered feelings life had left me with. Behind this shell I could perhaps ignore the pain and the loneliness and the grief of bereavement. But although it might provide some security I knew that at any moment my protection might crumble.

Life was not made easier for us by the fact that ' Mummy', as I came to call her, found married life was very different from the romantic picture she had always held. And no wonder! Post-war Britain proved to be a taxing environment in which to run a home and bring up a family. Long queues for rationed food, shortage of coal for heating, coupled with the many problems of managing the household of the college where Father now worked and where we now lived, combined to sap her strength.

Mummy was a remarkable Christian woman, a lively gifted public speaker, and blessed with great organizing ability. But although she could be the life and soul of the party, sending everyone into stitches with her funny stories and winning many friends through her generosity, she had a sharp tongue and could shrivel my sister and me to the size of a pinhead with her torrent of acid words. She also saw herself as Rebecca in Daphne du Maurier's famous novel, feeling constantly under Mother's shadow, and so never allowed us to speak of her. In fact she hated to see Father talk alone with any of us. Consequently, although he had been through so much and been separated from us for so long, he never had the opportunity to share deeply with us. Ironically this was made harder by the fact that the only job he had been able to find was to be Principal of Livingstone College, in whose grounds he had courted Mother so long ago.

Many teenagers are unhappy. They grope to understand the world around them. They long for independence and adulthood, but these desires are in conflict with their painfully obvious inadequacy. My sense of isolation made me very insecure. I found it easy to put on a front, as I was doing well at school, and outwardly all appeared fine. But inwardly I felt desperately lonely. Father was engrossed by his responsibilities and (as I have explained) was pressurized into not being intimate with his children. As for Mummy, circumstances had forced her to leave school at fourteen, and she often gave the impression of despising academic achievement. 'Anything useful in life is achieved by practical people!' was the message I read in her attitude. So although I did well at school I received little praise for my achievements.

But as I look back, I can see I was longing for love and appreciation and encouragement. I had been without my parents for those five crucial years in the Japanese prison camp and this had left an indelible mark on me. Missing the unconditional love which Mother had showered on me I sought to win approval through pleasing other people. My unconscious aim at Chefoo had been to please my teachers, and so gain the warmth of a sense of approval, even if it were a pale shadow of the real love I had once known. The same now happened with Mummy. I reacted to my longing for love by trying to please her. But in her character spontaneity was joined with unpredictability, and I soon concluded, to my horror, that this was impossible. She herself was longing for freely given love from her new family but I was becoming more and more tied up into perfectionism in my desire to please. Consequently we disappointed each other again and again. Deep hurts developed between us, although that was far from what either of us wanted.

I could not appreciate it at the time, but their marriage was under strain. The man she had married was sixty years old; he had been through appalling trauma and was still taxed to the limit of his strength with present demands. On their wedding day Father broke out in a mass of boils and Mummy spent that first evening attending to his pus-filled sores. Their honeymoon ended abruptly with the news that Rob, my oldest brother, had attempted suicide after experiencing the strains of Japanese prison and then having to adjust to life in England. From then on he was in and out of psychiatric hospitals for many years.

In addition Father and Mummy were completely opposed temperamentally. Father was steady and strong, with the accuracy and carefulness necessary for a surgeon. Mummy was vivacious and imaginative, and would not hesitate to use a touch of exaggeration to make a story more vivid. She loved variety and surprises. He was happy to get through another day, and then collapse by the fire. Many would have said at this time that they were incompatible: there was no way they could be happy together.

Yet God in his grace kept them together. It was their strong conviction born out of their Christian faith which made them

refuse to contemplate separation or divorce. They had made their
promises before God. They could not go back on that fact. Yet
pain and misunderstanding frequently flooded the house, making
the tension almost unbearable. Every month or so Mummy
would go for a long week-end to Devon where her parents and
a very understanding sister lived. These short breaks must have
been like oases to her hurting spirit.

I would escape by burying myself in books. 'Books are so much
more predictable than people,' I would think with a sigh of relief.
Then some new incident would jolt me back into the real world.

As they moved on through the years, God graciously helped
Father and Mummy in their life together. But it required hard
work as they struggled through years of intermittent joy and
misunderstanding. The strain finally caught up on Father and he
had a breakdown. Six months in hospital and electric shock
treatment helped a little. Mummy found a Christian psychiatrist,
a rarity in those days. His loving insight aided her greatly in
understanding Father's temperament. She began to learn to
accept him for what he was. Yet her strong character always
dominated. From being a strong, capable doctor, he became
much more placid. The friends who came to our house were
largely her friends. And as he grew older he learnt to be content
with simple domestic tasks. Through it all, Father's humility and
gentleness shone increasingly brightly.

In old age they mellowed into a beautiful couple, deeply fond
of each other and grateful for each other's love and care. Our
three children remember only this stage of their grandparents'
life. They looked forward to our visits to Granny and Grandpa
Hoyte. The atmosphere was always warm and welcoming.
Granny would often have prepared a surprise for them and was
full of fun and fresh ideas of things to do, so the children were
never bored. Both of them loved their grandchildren deeply and
thoroughly enjoyed our visits.

I have often thanked God for the model of Christian marriage
which these two servants of Christ gave. They made their vows

without realizing the strains that would come their way. Besides
their differences of temperament, they brought to their marriage
vastly different outlooks and experiences, with Father having
spent over thirty years in China. Their situation was far from easy
in the difficult post-war years. Having to make a home and earn
a living for their large family added to their problems. I believe
if they had not been Christians they would have given up on
their marriage. But both of them loved Jesus Christ and above
all else they wanted to please him. This enabled them to pray
together and to work for a common goal. At the same time
through their struggles the Lord was working the beauty of his
own character into their lives. As a result, many came to them
for counsel and refreshment. And I too enjoyed my monthly
visits to them in their old age, and received much love and
warmth.

What will you do with your life?

During my teenage years a friend called Beth made her home
with us. Her parents were missionaries in Brazil. Separated from
them for years. she also often felt pangs of loneliness. The
virulent tropical diseases and the lack of English-speaking
schools made it almost impossible for missionary parents in that
country to keep their children with them. Hurt and angry at
the way life had treated her, Beth one day poured out her
pent-up emotions to an older person. The reply was blunt. 'Yes,
it's true. You have suffered all these things. But what are you
going to do with it now? Are you going to sit forever in a pool
of self-pity? Or are you going to make something with your
life? The choice is up to you!'

These words were true for me too. Indeed, they are true for
everyone, as none of us has the perfect upbringing. I grew to see
that while everyone has hurts and scars; we also have a choice.
We can remain imprisoned in the pain of our past, nursing anger

and resentment at what has happened, or we can make a new start in our lives with God's help. This new start can then lead to blessing spreading out to others all around us.

But although the advice to Beth was sound, I did not find it easy to face this challenge and begin to take responsibility for my own life. My Christian faith helped to keep me steady through the years growing up into young adulthood. Here was something which I instinctively felt was rock solid. Perhaps in some ways I was too timid ever to think of abandoning it. Yet as various tests came with the passage of time, God proved himself utterly trustworthy and the Bible showed itself to be completely reliable. I searched out books to confirm my faith: books on archaeology which reinforced biblical history, books which demonstrated the reliability of the New Testament, and others which gave evidences for Christ's resurrection. In my own life too I was seeing answers to prayer which encouraged me to know that God was truly there, and that he cared personally for me.

My parents helped me too. We went to church together as a family on Sundays. At supper each evening Father would read a passage from the Bible, comment helpfully on it, and then pray. They encouraged us to join a Bible class on Sunday afternoons, and later to teach in Sunday School ourselves. And they backed me up when I started a Christian Union at my school. So I grew up, a mixture of timidity and growing confidence. I was beginning to feel more secure, and yet there remained an ache deep down inside, resulting from losing Mother. At this stage I knew no way of lancing this hurt.

God used Mummy to challenge me for overseas mission, and my 'call' seemed to be confirmed through a youth evening at our church. The vicar spoke on 'You are not your own, for you were bought with a price,' (1 Cor. 6:19,20). I realized for the first time that I was a Christian mainly for what I could get. Now God was saying, 'Christianity is more than that. You belong to me! I have done so much for you that now I have the right over your life.' I knew that either I must make Jesus Christ complete Lord of my life, or I must give it all up. There was to be no half-way: it was all or nothing.

As I cycled home the words went round and round in my head, following the rhythm of the pedals, 'You are not your own, for you were bought with a price.' That night I said, 'All right, Lord. I give myself totally to you. You are a loving Father, so I can trust you. It's not much to give you. I'm so unsure of myself, and so often tongue-tied when I want to speak about you. But here I am. Take me.' A deep assurance that God had heard my prayer came to me, and I felt certain that he wanted me to serve him somewhere as a missionary.

God took me back to Asia to serve with my parents' missionary society under its new name of the Overseas Missionary Fellowship, and in the setting of this new life some of the necessary healing began. In spite of Mummy's warmth and generosity she was too dominating a character, and I had found it impossible to blossom while still in her shadow. In a new country I could begin to try my wings and grow in self-confidence.

Martin and Marriage

More important for my path of healing than moving away from Mummy was God's gift of a life-partner, someone who loved me unconditionally. Martin appeared to see me through rose-tinted spectacles; although I could not believe half of what he said about me, it was so good to feel the warmth of his love. I was so unsure of my own heart that I led him a dance for a whole year, sometimes blowing hot, sometimes cold. But he steadfastly persisted; and it was wonderful when finally the matter was settled and we knew we belonged to one another. The Lord's loving healing of my childhood traumas continued gently through Martin's persistence in believing in me, and his deep commitment to me as a person.

While I had a family background of several generations of committed Christians, Martin's ancestors were Jewish. His parents had been baptized into the Christian church in order to be accepted as truly English but he was not brought up to know what it means to be a committed Christian. While studying at Oxford university he became aware of the emptiness of respectable middle-class expectations, and came into the experience of the glory of salvation and new life in Christ. This radically changed the course and purpose of his life. From then on he witnessed to his friends, both at university and at home, and many of them found Christ too. Mission became central to him.

Our first assignment after marriage was to the Karo Batak Church in North Sumatra. Here I experienced what it was really like to be involved in cross-cultural mission. God gave us an amazing privilege in working with this church. We learnt lessons we were to be thankful for many times in the future.

There had been remarkable progress in mission situations since my great-grandparents' time. They had been pioneer missionaries in a large area where there was not a single Christian. In my grandparents' day churches were already beginning to emerge. A generation later, my parents had struggled with the problem of how to help these new national churches stand on their own feet and be truly autonomous. Now Martin and I were privileged to be responsible to a fully indigenous group of churches and experience what it was like to be under their leadership.

One early experience stands out vividly. We had returned from a visit to a neighbouring village and reported enthusiastically to our local Christian friends that the people there were ripe for evangelism. Their reply was blunt. 'Missionaries should be under the table' – by which they meant, 'We don't want you leading anything!'

This was actually part of the basis on which we had been invited to work in Kabanjahe, their central market town. The Karo Bataks had experienced a paternalistic attitude from their former colonial missionaries, who kept all leadership, decision-making and finances in their own hands. After being suddenly forced into independence, the church vowed they would never have missionaries again. Now, a good ten years later, they were willing to take on an OMF couple as an experiment. But they made three strict stipulations. We must be willing to live in the house of their choice. We were not to give financially to the church beyond what an ordinary member could afford. And we were forbidden to speak in any meeting unless invited.

The housing stipulation was made so that we might live on a level with ordinary people, not more comfortably as earlier missionaries had done. Indeed, this was the normal OMF policy and we gladly fell in with it. In fact we added something else ourselves: we decided never to use anything which the local people did not have. So we left our camera in our suitcase, along with the flannelgraph and other teaching aids. We had no refrigerator or washing machine. We rode bicycles rather than owning a car. All of this was because we sensed they had relied too much on missionaries. They had a tendency to feel 'foreigners have better equipment, and therefore they can do things'. Instead, we constantly urged them, 'You know the language. You're much more effective than us. Go ahead and we'll be right behind you. Anything we can do, you can do better.'

The financial rule was laid down because they knew that money wields power. Previously over 90% of their finance had come from Holland. When the Dutch missionaries were forced to leave, no more money could be sent. This nearly brought the church to its knees. They determined that never again would they be dependent on foreign aid!

Sadly, when we revisited our Karo Batak friends twenty years later we found they no longer maintained this attitude. The General Secretary's whole conversation with us focused on how he could tap money from foreigners. Apparently their high ideals had not withstood the pressures of western materialism. A smart new office block, built with overseas money, betrayed how strong those pressures could be. Indonesia was already developing into one of the Asian 'tiger economies'. But as I write in 1997, the vulnerability of its corrupt economic structures has led to financial collapse. Nevertheless, the danger still exists that the desire for material wealth could undermine the churches' commitment to Christ.

The third rule, that we were not to speak unless invited, was intended to prevent us from dominating through our teaching role and in the church discussions. Westerners are often too quick to speak as we are embarrassed by silence. But we were invited in order to serve, not to control in any way.

This situation was not without its frustrations. For instance, we were asked to start a young people's fellowship, but on condition that it must be held in the church, not in the comparative informality of our home. We felt very discouraged at our first few meetings with twenty or thirty young folk sitting on the front benches of a gloomy church large enough to seat a thousand people. But the Karo leaders wanted the youth to keep coming to church, and this was their way of imposing that.

Evangelism

Greater still was our frustration at the fact that no one responded to our plea to begin evangelism. We were firmly told we were not to do this – our job was teaching Christians. Yet we sensed there was a wide open opportunity for church planting. All we could do was pray, and wait, and teach in the evening home groups when we were invited. However, if we had initiated evangelism it would have been done in our western way. So many were ready to respond that probably we would have been able to plant a church. We might have been acclaimed as 'successful' missionaries. But the reaction of the Karo Batak Christians might well have been, 'Missionaries are good at such things. We'll leave it to them . . . and to a few people whom they inspire to go with them.' The work would then have been dependent on foreign workers.

As it was, our hands were tied until God moved in their hearts. Some while later at one memorable evening home group an elderly Bible teacher unexpectedly announced, 'I've had an idea! Our church ought to be doing evangelism.' He told each of the six home groups to choose a neighbouring village, and start work there. They should send out two members, and the rest of the group should pray. It transpired that some of our closest friends had relatives in the village we had visited. Through kinship ties, some of these relatives were 'junior' to them, and their home could be used for a meeting. It was the same in other villages. So within a couple of weeks six teams were moving out in evangelism, holding meetings in homes which were open to them. Crowds listened through the open doors and windows.

The teams soon discovered they knew little about evangelism and so asked us to teach them. This gave us the joy of training a group of highly-motivated people. From time to time Martin would go with them, but never regularly, so that they would always feel the responsibility was theirs. As they developed, several of them became brilliant evangelists, much better than we were. The training course folded up after some months just because they were too busy with all their evangelism. But that was a good reason for stopping!

Other Christians soon began to say, 'If the church in Kabanjahe can plant churches, we can do so too.' New teams sprang up all over the area. Things began to snowball with more and more Christians realizing they had a message to share, and experiencing the joy of leading others to Christ. God's Holy Spirit had guided to a much more effective method of evangelism than we would have proposed. The national Christians knew the culture and what was most appropriate. They did their church planting through evangelistic Bible discussion meetings in homes. In two years the Karo Batak church grew from 20,000 members to 25,000, and a new atmosphere of expectancy prevailed.

By God's grace it was the same with the youth group which had started so hesitantly. It soon grew so large that it would never have fitted into our home. Many young people experienced a radical change of life. I remember one work-worn mother coming timidly to visit us and saying, 'Thank you for teaching my son. He's so different now. He notices when I'm tired and is so helpful around the house.' God's miracles in changing lives became the talk of the town. In the coffee shops and in the market animated discussion hummed around this new movement. One minister told us it was impossible for him to go out on evangelism: so many people were coming to ask how they could become Christians that he could not leave the house!

A mass movement can also have its dangers. Although many people were radically changed, there was no doubt that others jumped on the band wagon. But the church rejoiced that they now had the right to teach them, so some of these too came to personal faith. The emerging problem was how to teach all these new believers so that they would be grounded in the Word of God and grow into mature Christians. As a basis, everyone was expected to attend home groups for instruction. Training classes for elders and deacons were held so that they could teach these home groups. We were often asked to go for several days to a village. 'If you will come for three days,' they would say, 'we will drop everything else and learn from you all day. Then in the evening we can hold evangelistic meetings.' Martin would sometimes be expected to teach for ten hours a day, they were so hungry to learn.

After we returned to Britain for our first furlough even more spectacular growth occurred. This came partly as a reaction to the Communists' attempted coup in October 1965. But the structures for that growth were already well developed so that the 20,000 Christians grew to 80,000 in the next four years.

Further spiritual lessons

Martin and I were learning too that our difficulties were the raw material for God's miracles. Again and again we faced problems beyond our control: baffling situations, lack of essential supplies, shortage of clean water etc., only to see our loving Lord working a miracle on our behalf. (I have described these encouraging events more fully in *God can be Trusted*.)

At the same time Martin and I were learning that it is often in weakness that God's power is most clearly seen. Martin became ill with asthma and for a long time we had no adequate treatment for it – the modern nasal inhalants were not available at that time in Indonesia. So he was often teaching in total weakness, gasping for breath, and wondering how he could survive the evening. I suffered from frequent colds and bouts of influenza. I remember vividly the first time we were both prostrate in bed, how our Christian neighbours came in and lovingly cared for us. They brought us food, swept and washed the floor, and did everything they knew. 'You are our guests', they assured us. 'We're responsible for you.' So it was that any feeling they had that missionaries are superhuman was quickly dispelled. In this way we learnt another advantage of working under a national church who felt answerable for our welfare.

This was underlined when anti-British riots broke out in the capital city at the time of 'Confrontation' with the newly-formed Malaysia. The British Consul sent a message saying we were to have bags packed and be ready to leave at a moment's notice. But our church leaders, who knew the situation in the hills much better than he did, reassured us. 'Don't worry,' they said. 'We're keeping an eye on things. We'll tell you what to do.' And they proved extremely reliable.

Martin and I were also learning the lesson that when things apparently go badly wrong the Lord is still in control. When we had first arrived in Sumatra our quarterly allowance from OMF HQ in Jakarta failed to arrive. (There was no proper banking system for transferring money and the post was notoriously unreliable.) The one OMF couple in the capital could not help us as they had no money to spare. 'I've enough to pay your fare on the three-hour bus journey,' he stated encouragingly. But we were faced with the stark prospect of setting up home in a distant town on the mountain plateau with no money at all!

Seeing some new Indonesian Bibles on a table, Martin suggested we should take them and see if we could sell them. 'Oh, they don't read in the mountains,' was the disheartening reply!

However, we took those six Bibles and when we produced them our first evening a couple were snapped up at once. The other four were sold in a day or two. We realized that, far from 'not reading', our Christian friends were hungry to learn. I used some of the money to buy food, and Martin used the rest to return to the capital and buy as many Christian books as he could afford, with as big a discount as he could wring out of the manager.

So began our book-selling ministry. It expanded so greatly over the months that soon we were not asking OMF Jakarta for money, but for more books. This helped us immensely in a time of crippling inflation, when our allowance would have lost 20–30 percent of its value in the time taken to transmit it. Moreover, nearly every week someone testified that through one of these books they had been converted or received some major blessing. Just inside our front door we kept two cardboard boxes covered with a cloth on which we displayed the books. Each Sunday as we preached in a different village we carried a large hold-all of books for sale. Usually most of them sold; but even more wonderful – our bag was still heavy, this time with produce from the village. They gave us rice, pineapples, eggs, flowers and once or twice even a squawking hen!

'You give us spiritual food,' they said. 'We want to repay you with what we have.' So again we were learning the joys of being vulnerable and needy, not the foreign missionaries who come only to give out of their largesse and wisdom.

What about our rights?

My parents had taught me to be content to live like those around us in China. Before sailing for Asia, all of us missionary candidates had read a book by Mabel Williamson called *Have we no Rights?* It was based on what Paul says in 1 Corinthians 9 about his rights as an apostle, and his willingness to give them all up for the sake of the gospel. Mabel Williamson looked in detail at many of the 'rights' one might expect: the right to normal standards of living, to ordinary safeguards of good health, to regulate one's private affairs, to privacy and so on. She challenged her readers: if they wished to be effective in cross-cultural mission they must be willing to give these up.

Martin and I planned our life and work in North Sumatra according to this pattern and we saw it bearing fruit. We took it for granted that, for a dedicated missionary, this was God's pattern. At the same time we also discovered the truths with which she ends her book:

> Christ had no rights . . . and I?
>
> A right to the 'comforts' of life? No, but a right
> to the love of God for my pillow.
>
> A right to physical safety? No, but a right
> to the security of being in his will.
>
> A right to love and sympathy from those around me? No, but the right
> to the friendship of the One who understands me better than I
>   do myself.
>
> A right to be leader among men? No, but the right
> to be led by the One to whom I have given my all, led as is a
>   little child
> with its hand in the hand of its Father.

A right to a home and dear ones? No, not necessarily, but a right to dwell in the heart of God.

A right to myself? No, but
oh! I have a right to Christ.'

I feel this was the attitude my great-grandparents, Royal and Eliza Jane Wilder, displayed when they sailed for India in 1846, little knowing what would happen to them. They held to these principles even through years of meagre results. Robert and Helene Wilder, my grandparents, also showed the same dedication in their consuming passion to see the world evangelized in their generation. My parents, Stanley and Grace Hoyte, were also willing to give up all comfort and professional status for love of their Lord and Saviour.

For Martin and me, our brief time among the Karo Bataks faced us with many difficulties and problems, far beyond our capacity to cope. But we came through feeling greatly privileged. We had made many wonderful friends, seen God miraculously answer prayer again and again, and above all experienced the moving of the Holy Spirit, setting a church on fire in spectacular numerical growth and changed lives.

In our different ways, each generation of the family has proved that sacrifice for God has gone hand in hand with the lavish generosity of God.

Chapter 8

Rich Experiences

Malaysia

Visa problems prevented our returning to Indonesia after our first home assignment, and so we were asked temporarily to pastor a small church in Malaysia. My main responsibilities changed now as we had two small children, Andrew and Margaret. In some ways this was the loneliest stage of my missionary career as I was largely tied to the home. To go out visiting church members in the heat, with both a toddler and also a baby squeezed into a tiny springless carry-cot, left me hot and flustered and unable to hold a proper conversation.

I often felt very frustrated by my comparative ineffectiveness as a missionary compared to what I had been privileged to do in Sumatra. But this was a crucial stage in the development of our children. My mother had given generously of her unconditional love and her unstinting time to all of her six children. She in turn had received a deep stability and self-confidence through the continual love of her mother throughout her growing years. A deep instinct told me that giving myself to laying a good foundation in my childrens' lives was my primary task at that time.

God provided opportunities for refreshment as well as caring for others. The army garrison in town owned a large open-air swimming pool and paddling pool where we were allowed to relax on days off. Set on the top of a green hill, it was surrounded by flowering scarlet hibiscus and scented frangipani. The site overlooked a helicopter field, and Martin and little Andrew had much fun together watching them take off and land.

The beautiful east coast town of Mersing was only two hours' drive away. We sometimes visited Malaysian friends there and relaxed in the comfort of their home. At other times we would drive out to the nearby hills and have a picnic and watch the chattering monkeys. Each year we made the long drive up to the Cameron Highlands to the OMF guest house for a holiday. Our mission's junior school was situated nearby in the cool of that healthy climate. We would take Andrew and Margaret to play with the children and meet the staff, in order to prepare them for becoming boarders there one day. Thankfully, in the end, they never had to be separated from us although, if they had been, this would have been the ideal place.

Knowing how easy it is for mothers of young children to become 'stale', Martin made sure I had my own ministry as well. Each Saturday afternoon he would look after Andrew and Margaret while I taught a Bible class. It was a privilege to teach the young people and get to know them a little.

As the months went by, our home became a centre of activity. Our small church consisted almost entirely of young people, and many dropped in to visit us and play with the children. Once a month we invited all who wished to come and stay with us for the weekend. Twenty or thirty mattresses could be put down in our huge attic. The two spare bedrooms could also sleep a good number of young people. The larger group, whether of boys or girls, would sleep in the attic. They would arrive after lunch on the Saturday, and we laid on a varied programme of teaching, fun and games, and worship. Costs were kept to a minimum with only the one main meal on Saturday evening and a light breakfast, so that nearly everyone could afford it. The few who were already working kindly contributed a little extra. Talking went on late into the night as these young Christians encouraged each other. Before breakfast small groups taught the new-comers how to have a regular time of meeting with God each day. These monthly mini-conferences deepened friendships and gave opportunity for the mature to develop teaching skills.

Training new missionaries

When the political situation between Britain and Indonesia improved, Martin and I expected to return to the land of our calling. But our mission leaders invited Martin instead to be the Superintendent of the Language School in Singapore. As we thought and prayed about it, this request confirmed the way our interest had been developing. We ourselves had only recently struggled with adapting to different cultures, moving between progressive Singapore, rural Sumatra and small-town Malaysia. Languages had been Martin's primary focus at university. Training new workers who had just arrived in Asia was a challenge we would enjoy. To bring the various language courses up-to-date would be right up Martin's street. So, after eighteen months in Malaysia, it was with enthusiasm that we moved to our new appointment.

Our two and a half years in this new role was a time of further learning and developing. As Andrew and Margaret grew older, I had more time to be directly involved in Christian ministry, especially as we employed Chinese women to look after all the children on site in the mornings. Martin was able to install a language laboratory which considerably improved the facilities and achieved better results. I utilized my artistic gifts on the decor of the house, getting all the bedrooms redecorated in pastel colours with matching curtains, and encouraging the gardener to grow a mass of beautiful flowers.

We thought we were doing well, and grew increasingly confident that training new missionaries was now God's calling for us. But we were young and inexperienced, and had little understanding of how to handle people and doubtless made many mistakes. As the time drew near for our second home assignment our mission leader called Martin to his office. Without any consultation Martin was told that someone else was to be given the language school. We must look for some other job in the mission. The shock of this news brought one of the hardest lessons we had to face.

In researching my family heritage I have come to see that our situation had some things in common with what my great-grand-parents faced. They felt that their mission leaders failed to talk openly with them or listen to their point of view, so that no relationship of caring oversight had been established. We too asked ourselves, 'If there were inadequacies in the way we led the language school, could they not have been discussed openly with us?' None of the Directors had made time to form a personal relationship with us. We had been expected to step into leader-ship after only a few years overseas without any relevant training. No one had drawn alongside us to help us develop into the job.

Royal Wilder's experience had left him hurt, deeply angry and resentful. When no one in authority would listen to him he poured out his anger in a torrent of self-justification. Apparently his angularity grew more pronounced the more his views were opposed. We too felt hurt to the quick, feeling we had been misjudged and misunderstood. We had to struggle against bitter-ness and a sense of injustice. We never considered going public over the clash as Royal did, or leaving OMF out of pique. But we gave notice that we were now open to invitations from other Christian movements. (I would not write about it now, except that by God's grace we have continued close relationships with the mission and I feel this event has valuable lessons.)

Besides the surprise and the hurt, we felt baffled as to our future guidance. God had seemed to be calling us into mission training. Yet the one job in mission training in OMF was now closed to us.

Our anguished hearts cried out: 'Have our leaders mistaken God's will? If so, how should we deal with this mess?' All we could do was to plead with God to bring good out of the situation, and on our part refuse to allow bitterness or anger to lodge in our hearts.

My parents too faced a sharp disagreement with their mission leaders at one time. Although they really wanted to remain in Chefoo where we six children were at school, they eventually acquiesced in the autocratic decision that they must go and lead the hospital in distant Lanchow. This crisis must have cost them a great deal; and huge repercussions flowed from it, reverberating in the lives of each member of our family. Christian leaders need to be very careful in making decisions about other peoples' lives.

All Nations Christian College

There followed eighteen months of uncertainty, during which Martin and I wondered if we had completely failed to sense God's will. But in the end God worked the situation out for good. At that time All Nations Christian College was being formed out of three smaller colleges. Its specific aim was to train people for cross-cultural mission. When they invited us to join the staff, we realized that this was what God had been preparing us for. This was why he had moved us on from city life in modern Singapore, to Bible teaching in large churches in rural Sumatra, and then on to small-town pastoring of a growing church in Malaysia. This was why we had been exposed to all the world's major religions during our ten years in Asia, so that we could train people going to many different countries. Here in All Nations Christian College we put down our roots, and for over twenty years were blessed and challenged and stretched.

The ANCC emphasis on holistic mission echoed strongly all that we had been learning in Sumatra. The situation there cried out for biblical teaching and training in the churches; these needed to flow out in evangelism and church planting if they were not to stagnate. The church planting generated a need for further teaching, which in turn overflowed into more evangelism. Theory and practice had been reflected in our youth meetings where we always had two talks. One was a biblical exposition. The other was on a practical subject such as 'relating to parents' or 'handling money'. Members of the youth group soon expressed their excitement in their new-found faith by coming with us on hospital evangelism. One of our young men from a neighbouring race went home in the vacation and planted a church in his Muslim village. He then found himself in the position of having to teach and lead that church.

All this exactly fitted the training at ANCC, which aimed to bring together biblical knowledge, theological truth, missiological insights, practical skills, spiritual development and pastoral understanding. All the courses were studied from a cross-cultural point of view, in order to remove western blinkers. With more than thirty different nationalities training together, there was a strongly multicultural atmosphere. ANCC pioneered the study of non-western theologies and guest lecturers from many different countries were invited to share their expertise with the college.

In my years on the staff of ANCC I always felt I gained far more than I gave out. Attending the lectures of other members of staff gave me a deeper biblical insight. Working as part of a team taught me much about group dynamics. And the pastoral studies course began to give me an understanding of my own background, and also how to pastor and counsel. I found it a great privilege too to be given responsibility for a tutorial group.

A missionary in Britain

Returning to the UK varied, but did not abolish, the 'missionary' heritage. I knew that my calling to be a missionary was not abrogated by our remaining in Britain. Ministry in this country would also require cross-cultural understanding and building bridges. We found ourselves in a small village in Hertfordshire, faced with choosing between a very traditional Anglican Church or a tiny Free Church which was slowly dying. Initially we joined the evangelical Anglican Church in a neighbouring town so that the children could go to Sunday School. But I kept feeling that the Lord had placed us in this particular village for a purpose. It was easy to get in a car and travel to a church which we enjoyed, but what about the challenge on our doorstep?

Brenda and I met one day on the High Street. We began to pray and plan together – how could we reach the women in the village? Brenda was very gregarious and knew lots of people. So we started informal coffee evenings, at which a variety of speakers talked about their faith and their work. It became apparent that some of the ladies were spiritually open, and an evangelistic Bible study was started. At the same time we kept praying that the Lord would either bless the vicar with new spiritual life, or move him! After some years there was a noticeable change in his life.

One of the young wives asked the vicar to hold family services, as her three children would be bored attending traditional Morning Prayer. He had never seen a family service but we obtained his permission for ANCC students to hold one once a month, between the early morning Communion and the 11 o'clock service. This soon became the growing point of the church. And when at last an evangelical vicar was appointed this 10 a.m. service became the main event of the week.

As a village church we have had our periods of discouragement and set-back, as well as times of consolidation and advance. But we can praise God for bringing a vibrant living witness to his grace into our community. A system of shared ministry has been developed. At one time we had a team of three men and three women, some ordained and some lay, sharing the ministry of leading and preaching. I trained as a lay minister, grateful that my Father had always encouraged women to exercise their gifts to the full. This team ministry became an encouragement for all the congregation to develop their gifts, and many more people became involved in the activities of the church. At present we have a warm-hearted and gifted lady curate who has moved us all forward by setting up Alpha groups and enlisting many members as group leaders and hospitality carers. In Sumatra we saw the church growing because ordinary Christians took responsibility both for evangelism and for teaching. It has been good to see the same lesson being applied here in Britain.

Family Life

There are various reasons why part of the 'heritage' of a missionary family has often been tensions or distance between parents and children. Since both Martin and I were the youngest in our families we had never learnt to relate to children, let alone babies! Overshadowed by five siblings, my aim in youth had been to grow up and appear mature, taking my place among the other adults. But then in a remote mountainous area of Sumatra I had to face caring for a new-born baby with no support from welfare state, health visitor or even another western missionary nearby.

During those early months I had been extremely tense. Although our local friends plied me with advice, I never knew whether to take it. I remember clearly the sigh of relief with which I deposited seven-month-old Andrew on Mummy's lap when at last our ship docked in Southampton. Before marrying my Father she had helped care for countless missionaries' children whose parents were stationed overseas. Her relaxed attitude with children helped me to begin to overcome my fears.

Margaret's birth in the UK had formed a welcome contrast. With relaxation classes beforehand and surrounded by skilled medical care, her arrival proved far more enjoyable. After those months of family support I felt more confidence in returning to Asia with two small children.

Martin and I had always shared the responsibility of our children. We had a big advantage because, as missionaries, we were both 'working from home'; so the children saw a great deal of their father while they were small. He was far better than I at romping with them and teasing and having fun. I still felt very inadequate in many areas of my life. Our Christian principles provided clear guidelines by which to bring them up; and Andrew and Margaret knew real security and love in those early days.

Although I recognized that my main priority was the family, I sometimes experienced tension, because I was not doing 'real missionary work'. But Martin gave me great support, and indeed we both felt strongly that while the children were small they must be my priority. However it was a great relief when we were back in the UK and Ruth arrived. I was not yet teaching at ANCC, so I could give myself completely to making a home, caring for the needs of the family and enjoying each one. I am so thankful that I was spared the necessity of working full time, so I could always be at home when they came in from school and listen to them chattering about the day's activities. Martin was usually at home by six o'clock as we live only a mile away from the college and we then would all sit down to conversation over an evening meal and share in homework or family games.

As he became better known, Martin received an increasing number of invitations and so was away from home more and more. Twice I had to organize the childrens' long summer holidays by myself, and I did not find this easy. But the Lord made it up to us by giving us wonderful family holidays all together in other years. Martin feels that he did not help as much with Ruth's upbringing as he did with the other two. However, in spite of this they have a very good relationship together now. It was taxed to the limit when (surprise! surprise!) she was in her teens. For some time she dressed all in black, judged everyone scathingly by the music they preferred, argued endlessly over pocket money, and wanted to go out with boys whom we felt were entirely unsuitable – all of which will be familiar to many parents of teenagers. Thankfully it was only a 'passing phase', and her Christian commitment and the family bonding won through.

We were saddened to see Andrew gradually moving away from his Christian upbringing. There were no other boys his age in the youth group at church; and reluctantly we decided we should not force him to come with us if he did not wish to. It was not easy to maintain good relationships, as the very basis of our lives was completely different but we recognized that each child must be free to develop as they wish. To try to restrain them would only drive them further away. But it was painful allowing him to make his own choice and seeing how far apart our paths were diverging. Today Andrew is a successful lawyer who has held responsible jobs in Bombay and Jakarta and we are so glad that we really enjoy each other and that the communication between us is so good.

Having Christian friends has made things easier for the girls. As they came up against different moral issues at school or on TV we were able to discuss together the Christian viewpoint. So their faith has been strengthened. All the same there was a big clash with Margaret. At the end of her first year at Cambridge she announced she wanted to leave and get married. We had not been happy with her becoming engaged before university. 'You've hardly met any suitable men yet. Leave it a little longer!' had been our reaction. Now she appeared to be throwing away the wonderful opportunity of studying at Cambridge, just because her fiancé was starting a new church and said he needed her at his side! We found it hard to believe that our loving Christian daughter was not willing to follow our advice, and had such a strong mind of her own.

Thankfully, all our discussions together were steeped in prayer and the bonds of family love held. After much pain and heart-searching a compromise was reached. If she could get a transfer to the local college, and could continue her degree course, and if the grant could be transferred too, then we would agree. With her gifts and charm she negotiated all the necessary interviews, and within six weeks she was married. Aged twenty, she coped amazingly with being a new bride, running a home, taking on the responsibilities of a pastor's wife, and starting in the second year of a new university. Looking back, we can see that the challenge brought out the best in Margaret. She seemed to mature overnight and managed all her conflicting roles extremely well. The church also has flourished.

As each of our children has grown up, it has been a particular joy to find our relationship developing from that of a 'parent with child' to deep adult love and friendship. We each have our own lives but greatly appreciate and enjoy each other. And now two grandchildren blow us kisses over the telephone and hug us excitedly when we visit!

Challenges to grow

Our children develop in different ways from us and I recognize that our grandchildren will surely face a very different world. Life involves us all in a process of change and development and I too had to face the fresh challenges of my own generation. My parents and grandparents had struggled to know how to develop the early stages of church life in Asia. I needed to acquire other skills for a church which was more established. Training to be a Christian Listener has opened new aspects of spirituality for me. The Christian Listener movement, founded by Anne Long, who is a dear friend of ours, trains people in the basic pastoral skill of listening – to others, to oneself and to God.

Listening

Listening to others has started me on the path of counselling. It is one of the greatest privileges I know to be able to minister to the deep needs of another person and to be a channel through whom God may heal them. In our broken society today there appears to be an increasing number of hurting people. If they can share their feelings honestly with another person who listens attentively this can have a healing effect. The Lord has been teaching me how to minister to such people in prayer. As Jesus' presence becomes a reality for them, and as he touches the deepest recesses of their personality, so the healing comes.

Leading a tutorial group at ANCC has involved me in many kinds of counselling. Students need to talk over guidance for the future and discuss relationships with their parents or their sending churches. They have been grateful for help with their studies, and for challenge to their spiritual life and growth. All of these have had an effect on me, providing a stimulus to grow spiritually and consequently having more to give to others.

As I have learned to listen to people, so I have gained a new sense of the importance of *listening to God*. Learning to listen to God more clearly has brought a fresh dynamic to my spiritual life. Through looking at the ways God communicated with people in the Bible, I have been alerted to hear him speak, not just through Scripture as my upbringing had taught, but in many other ways also. As 'the heavens declare the glory of God' so his work in nature can be his voice. Music, song and dance can help us to hear him through our senses. Occasionally God has used dreams to speak to me. His voice can be heard through photographs, his glorious splendour seen in majestic mountains or his deep compassion in scenes of human tragedy or need. Other people too can be the voice of God: to challenge, encourage, correct or teach. At times the Lord has used a prophecy to confirm a present course of action or to move me into new paths. Of course all these means of communication must be tested against the final authority of Scripture to discern how much of their content is inspired by God.

The growing desire to hear God's voice and be closer to him has led me into different ways of meditating on the Bible. I have found the slow reading of a passage to be very fruitful, as I savour each word, sucking out its richness like a bee sucking honey from a flower. I spent a whole week meditating on Christ's amazing words, 'As the Father has loved me, so have I loved you' (John 15:9). These wonderful words have the power to dispel any tinge of tiredness or depression!

Meditating on a theme throughout Scripture has proved very enriching. I think of 'the desert' and see it as a place of hardship and testing. As I picture it, I recall tales of missionaries crossing the Gobi desert and these fill in additional details with their stories of mirages and dancing 'dust devils'. But it was in the desert that our Lord won a decisive victory over Satan and the power of God's word was experienced.

Real-life experience of symbols found in Scripture can also reveal deep meaning. To gaze at a steady candle glowing in a dark room brings a fresh awareness of Jesus as 'the light of the world'. A simple bowl of water and a towel can speak volumes, as can a shepherd's crook or five smooth pebbles.

One of the most vivid ways I have found to feel Christ's presence is in using what is called 'Ignatian' meditation. This entails first praying to the Holy Spirit to guard one's mind and quicken one's imagination, then reading a gospel story. Instead of thinking of the event as happening two thousand years ago, one places oneself within the story, thus meeting Jesus, who was there in the biblical story, and who is still here with us – 'the same yesterday, today and for ever'.

I remember meditating in this way on Christ washing his disciples' feet. The Upper Room became very vivid. The steaming food was placed on the table and the disciples began to gather round. Because I too was a disciple I joined them in my spirit. Then in my heart I saw the Lord of Glory strip off his outer garment, take a bowl of water and a towel, and begin to wash his disciples' feet. He moved slowly around the room until he actually knelt in front of me, his broad shoulders bowed at *my* feet! How could it be? The emotions of gratitude, love and protest surged within me. And yet I knew it was true. God himself in love and humility kneels to serve us. How can we do anything else but respond in gratitude for the rest of our lives?

It was in learning to *listen to myself* that I found a deeper level of healing from my childhood traumas. I had always been taught that Christians should not be too engrossed with themselves. We should think of others and care for them. This is true. However, unhealed wounds from the past often limit our ability to give effective care.

During a Pastoral Studies lecture I suddenly became aware of a deep hole of blackness inside me. It still remained, in spite of years of Christian ministry and the love of husband and children. As I asked timidly for prayer ministry, my feelings suggested strongly that this darkness was due to my deep sense of inadequacy in relating to my step-mother. All her sharp criticisms and the times I had failed her came vividly back to me. But when we asked the Holy Spirit to highlight whatever wounded memory he would like to touch, I suddenly remembered the day I was told that Mother had died. With the help of those who ministered to me, I could see again the headmaster's room and the six of us brothers and sisters standing in front of him. I felt again the numbness and the pain as the news was broken – the awful sense of unreality. Then in response to the prayers of my counsellors, and with the eye of faith, I was enabled to sense the presence of God himself coming into the room. What a relief to run towards him and to be gathered closely in his arms as he held me securely! God's loving presence reached further into the inner recesses of my personality than I had ever known before. Through this prayer ministry I felt God's healing and his unconditional love. I knew it would never change. It would always be there.

I have also received prayer ministry at other times, dealing with my relationship to Mummy and with other hurts. I am deeply grateful for the reality of the touch of God. He can truly heal the broken-hearted and bind up our wounds when we come to him. But sometimes we cannot experience this on our own. God often uses other Christians to bring this healing to us. He wants us to share one another's burdens, not to struggle on alone.

Present opportunities

These listening skills and experiences were something new, added after the apparent end of a 'missionary' career. But Martin and I have been grateful for the opportunity to keep in touch with Christians world-wide. After twenty-four years of being linked to All Nations Christian College, Martin and I are now engaged in a free-lance travelling ministry. Something similar happened to my grandfather. He too was led into wider travel. In his student ministry he was not only based in Britain and in USA, but visited many countries throughout Europe, from Scandinavia in the north, Spain and Portugal in the west, to France and Italy and on into Eastern Europe. Later life saw him responsible for the missionaries across a wide area of the Middle East.

Invitations to minister in other countries came to Martin even in our early days at ANCC. As the number of invitations grew he became increasingly busy. One five-week Easter break found him in five different countries. The pace of life seemed to have become too pressurized. So we sensed the Lord telling us to leave ANCC when we reached the age of sixty, and to give ourselves to this wider work.

Many different requests come our way. At the moment we have three fixtures in the year which allow us some stability in an otherwise constantly changing programme: a Missions School in Sweden, a somewhat similar one in Norway, and a very different mission training establishment in Korea. Recently we have been privileged to minister to the WEC missionaries in the Gambia, the Summer Institute of Linguistics team in Senegal, to OMF missionaries both in tribal and in Muslim work in the Philippines and to the International Church in Dakha, Bangladesh. We feel we have learned so much from these different ministries – each mission has its own particular character.

War-torn Afghanistan showed us the horrors of civil war and the courage of Christ's servants who have remained through it all. A visit near Chernobyl to train Ukrainian missionaries highlighted the disasters that follow in the wake of pollution, and yet how God can still bless his people there with a vision for mission. Kazakhstan demonstrated some of the problems when a newly opened and very responsive country is flooded by Christian workers, often with little regard for national Christians. Yet in spite of our mistakes, God builds his church. China has clearly showed that nothing can separate us from the love of God. Indeed, he can bring good out of evil, as the fantastic growth of the church there demonstrates.

We feel greatly enriched through having Christian friends in many different countries and also through mixing with very diverse groups. Invitations to speak at a wide variety of churches, conferences and student groups in Britain keeps us on our toes and allows us to see what God is doing. Our two daughters play a full part in the strongly charismatic Pioneer churches, and it is a privilege to minister to them at times. We ourselves have gained much from their deep commitment to Jesus Christ, their strong emphasis on building personal relationships and their freedom of expression in worship. Our own preference is for quieter, more meditative services, where space is given for silence, and the beauty of lighting, texture and colour enhances the sense of the presence of God. We would also want to emphasize a ministry of biblical as well as prophetic exposition.

Perhaps it is our cross-cultural experience in many different countries which enables us to move between these various groups, and feel at ease with all who love Jesus Christ. The body of Christ is rich in its diversity, and there are always truths we can learn from each other, and new experiences to challenge and develop us. Martin and I continue to be enriched by the legacy we receive from all God's people, not just from our own family.

BIBLIOGRAPHY
for chapters 7 & 8

Goldsmith, Elizabeth *God can be Trusted* (OM, 1974, 1984, 1996)
Goldsmith, Martin *Life's Tapestry* (OM, 1997)
Long, Anne *Listening* (Darton, Longman and Todd, 1990)
Oakley, Nigel *The story of Easneye* (All Nations Christian College, 1997)
Williamson, Mabel *Have we no right?* (Chicago: Moody Press, 1957)

Chapter 9

The Next Generation

While the children were growing up I had a striking poster in the kitchen with the caption, 'Give them Roots and Wings.' This slogan summarized what is needed for healthy family growth.

The first requisite is a stable foundation into which their developing *Roots* can penetrate and gain a firm hold. This was not easy to accomplish within our peripatetic missionary career. During Andrew's early childhood we lived in six different homes situated in four different countries! But our children have always known that 'home' depended, not on the house we lived in, but on the family being together and pulling together. We also thank God that since returning to the UK we have not had to move house. Andrew, Margaret and Ruth have been able to grow up steadily through junior and secondary school, building good friendships and learning to relate to others.

But the strength of the foundation we have offered comes not simply from our own personal qualities and efforts but from its grounding in God's revelation. The Bible is a consistent, reliable guide which can act as arbitrator when personalities clash and want to pull in opposite directions. Attempting to make Jesus Christ the head of our home and the joy and goal of our life has provided a solid centre of gravity, giving stability through storm or calm.

Yet at the same time we have known that Andrew, Margaret and Ruth must try out their own *Wings*. They must be free to develop their own personalities and make their own choices. We may not always approve of their decisions. But we have tried to

be constantly there in the background, loving, supporting and
ready to discuss situations when asked.

The 'empty nest syndrome' affects people in various ways. I
remember when Margaret, aged 19, was knocked off her bicycle
during her first year at university. I felt a sharp pang when she
phoned her fiancé Roger, who lived nearly three hours' drive
away, rather than Martin and me. We lived so much closer and
would have come at once when needed. My heart ached: 'She
doesn't belong to us any more!'

In a sense this was true. She had given Martin and me such
joy as she grew up, and there had been a growing sense of
companionship as she matured. Now we had to learn to be
willing to give her up. Of course she would always belong as
part of our family – but now in a different way. The family was
expanding through the formation of a new unit. Stretching can
often be painful, but it would only be by letting her go that warm
relationships could still continue to deepen and, more impor-
tantly, that she could be free to develop as God wanted her to
do. Families belong to God, not to parents.

I have asked Andrew, Margaret and Ruth if they would
contribute to my saga. They form the next generation. What will
they pass on to their children? Their contributions show how
varied their personalities are. At present Margaret and Ruth share
the spiritual and missionary vision of the family, while Andrew's
approach to life is very different. We are thankful for the good
relationships with each one.

Andrew is carving out for himself a successful career as a
solicitor. He has returned to his roots in that he loves the life-style
in Asia and will probably continue working overseas. For a year
he delighted in working in Jakarta, much enjoying being in the
land of his birth and sensing his Indonesian roots. He even made
a pilgrimage to his birth-place in North Sumatra. While working
full-time for a major international bank, he made time to learn
the language and was soon amazingly fluent. He has a zest for

life and mixes easily, making close friends with local people. Although he had no particular intention of returning to the family's Indian roots, he has also worked for several years in Bombay and feels very much at home there. While developing strong wings of his own, his roots still run deep.

Margaret, who has a heart for mission, recognizes that Britain is now far from being a Christian country; there is a need for church planting in the UK. As a church leader, she sees her role not just in pastoring and teaching Christians, but also in the primary task of the evangelization of her own generation. So the slogan of her great-grandparents is now being worked out at home as well as overseas. Just as her great-grandparents found their Presbyterian background too traditional and restrictive, so Margaret left her Anglican roots and found new life and flexibility in the new charismatic churches.

Ruth also has followed Margaret in her approach to church life, being an active member of the church which Margaret and Roger founded. However, her heart for mission is expressed in her desire to respond to the problems of poverty that confront all Christians, both overseas and in our own country. She recognizes the strong theme of justice that runs throughout the Bible, and is working to awaken the churches to be faithful to their calling. She feels that the culture of consumerism and materialism can easily blind us to our responsibilities.

Their husbands both come from families who did not go to church. Each of them vividly exemplifies the possibility of taking the difficult initial step of faith which breaks with the past and thus makes starting a new family line possible.

Roger, Margaret's husband, had left school at sixteen and being into Heavy Metal founded a club called 'the Rock Soc' where bikers and others would meet in a pub to drink and listen to this music. Drugs were freely passed around, although Roger did not often take them. Then his girl-friend found her life falling to pieces. She became anorexic and grew desperate. Finally she

said, 'I've got to *do* something – I'm going to try God. Either
you give it a go with me, or we'll have to break up.' After some
weeks during which they gained nothing from the girl-friend's
anglo-catholic church, Roger suggested they try an evangelical
Anglican church to which he had taken himself for a time several
years before.

On their first Sunday a rather large older woman announced
that there was no one to run the church football team. If nobody
could be found, she would have to do it herself. Roger found
the thought of her as the coach so incongruous that he volunteered on the spot. So he was hurled into becoming one of the
youth leaders before he knew anything much about the Christian
faith.

For a year he compromised, deep into his music and drink.
He would often turn up on a Sunday morning far from sober,
his hair soaked in beer from last night's party. Wisely the youth
leader did not directly confront him, but let him absorb the
Christian teaching week by week. Then one day, with a twinkle
in his eye, he asked Roger to lead the study next week. The
subject was to be 'alcohol'. Roger went home armed with a list
of verses to look up. At last he realized that getting drunk was a
sin, and that he must be totally committed to God or give it all
up. There could be no middle way.

Amid the deafening heavy metal music he started to witness
for Christ. A 'Jesus is Supernatural' T-shirt blazoned the change
which had come over him. Gradually many of his friends became
Christian too. They would gather in the same pub on Saturdays
for the Rock Soc and then on Sundays for a Christian meeting.
The Holy Spirit's power came upon them, and they saw many
lives dramatically saved and people delivered from the oppression
of drugs and the occult.

It was around this unlikely core that Revelation Church in
Chichester was formed.

Ruth's husband, Greg, had struggled through very difficult
youth experiences which developed in him a deep sensitivity for

the underprivileged and those who felt on the fringes of society. As a teenager he had known what it was to be in trouble with the police, to be expelled from school, and to experience the pain of his parents' divorce. Experimenting with drugs led him to explore eastern religions, mysticism and neo-paganism. In his increasing despair he explored one after another of the escape avenues which modern culture offers. But none of them met his need. Deep in his heart he felt angry with God and angry with those around him.

Several years passed, during which matters only grew worse. Finally, in desperation, he asked a young Christian leader to pray for him. This resulted in a four hour struggle as gradually each part of his past life was surrendered to the Lord. Since then the path of healing and spiritual growth has taken time, but it has changed him into a young man wholly dedicated to God, sensitive to those who are marginalized and apparent failures, and deeply committed to serving others.

As their stories will show, the ministries of Ruth and Margaret have been influenced both by their own background and by that of their own husbands. But the following pages also show how the distinctive personality and character of each has led them into new paths.

With their husbands, they aim to be on the cutting edge of Christian witness in Britain today, while ministering in other countries too. Revelation Church, founded by Roger, Margaret and their friends, appeals strongly to people in our post-modern society. Since the church began some ten years ago it has grown by leaps and bounds. Much of its strength lies in its vision, the warm relationships of the members and their culturally relevant worship. While playing a full part in this fellowship Ruth and Greg have also developed their own gifts and ministry.

In their varied accounts I have left each of the three of them free to say whatever they want. But the 'roots and wings' are clearly visible.

Speaking Personally . . .

Andrew

Asked whether he believed in the gods, a Greek philosopher replied: 'It's a difficult question and life is short.'

I was born on a Sunday morning, in the Chinese Year of the Rabbit, in a small hospital on a rubber estate in North Sumatra, Indonesia.

A *feng shui* master told me that I am like a rabbit, which leaves its burrow in the early hours of the morning to go in search of fresh grass. Because of that, he advised that I shouldn't work in the country where I was born – but I am writing this in my apartment in Indonesia looking out over the fumes and traffic. The *feng shui* master said that, unless I had long hair, I would not get married – and I have just had another short haircut!

My mother has told me that I was born as the first notes of the Sunday morning hymn were heard. Perhaps she saw that as having some significance. Perhaps it was part of her wish for what I would become.

But events and stories are capable of many interpretations, and perhaps are better left without having a pattern or interpretation pushed on to them. The most arresting incidents and the best stories need no interpretation. They are what they are. They stand self-contained, beautiful in themselves. I think life is like that. No gods or fairies are needed to make it complete. Life is short.

So, a few stories: I'm five years old in the first event I can remember. I'm the luckiest child in the world: living in Singapore, where my parents ran a missionary language school, surrounded by loving parents and their kind students whom I thought of as my 'uncles' and 'aunts'. And I'm nut-brown in the sun without a care in the world. I fell from a small tree. I didn't hurt myself but I cried, waiting for attention. No one came. Then I cried from irritation and because it was my right to be petted and kissed. And still no one came. And so I stopped and felt hard and angry and determined. I said I'd never cry again. I said I didn't want to be spoilt. I would be tough and independent.

Behind the missionary language centre where we lived lay the 'Jungle' and, at the top of the hill, what we called 'the Rich Man's House'. I never went there, and never wanted to, but I knew it must be vast and gleaming white, with perfectly symmetrical pillars. Like heaven. But the edges of the 'jungle', with its big tropical plants, was enough to keep me amused. Our gardener, Kebun, was a wonderful taciturn old man, who propped his antique bicycle under the banana trees at the back of the house and ate his meals wrapped in banana leaves held together with a twig. I would lie on the grass in the shade while he picked *rambutan*, a delicious Malaysian fruit. He caught vivid green snakes with bright eyes, which he'd hold up on two sticks for me to watch. Daddy used to catch snakes too, but he'd kill them, crushing their tiny heads with a spade. In the morning all that remained of that beautiful twisting snake was an ants' heap. My sister almost stepped on a snake one night, while reaching for the *Childrens' Illustrated Bible* to read a bed time story. It was squeezing the life out of a house lizard which had turned a mouldy yellow colour.

At the end of each day, my parents would read stories to me before turning out the light. They were wonderful, exotic stories: some nights they were Bible stories, some nights fairy stories. Almost all of them fascinated me. Whether any were true didn't make any difference.

Although I lead a very separate life from the rest of my family, we have much in common despite our differences in beliefs. At my age – 33 – my parents were living in Indonesia too. They were working as missionaries in North Sumatra. I'm a lawyer for an international bank. If I believed in God, I'd have liked to be a missionary too.

Here, in Indonesia, I am a Christian, as anyone who doesn't subscribe to any one of the five recognized religions – Islam, Protestant Christianity, Catholicism, Hinduism and Buddhism – must be a Communist and therefore a dangerous subversive. Elsewhere, I describe myself as an atheist, an atheist in the same way that most people describe themselves as Christian, when they think there's probably a god, but they're not sure, and are still open to being proved wrong. When I was in the Territorial Army, I was summoned to see my Commanding Officer and was told to change what was written on my dog-tag to 'Church of England', as there were to be no atheists in his regiment.

This week I went back, for the first time, to the place where I was born. It was a strange, disquieting thought to picture my mother in labour there, in all that pain, with all that love, giving birth to me. I know that there is no way that I can repay what my parents have done for me. Whatever little I do is insignificant, particularly as I cannot give them the thing that they appear to want most, which is that I should believe in their religion. But the rules of their religion make no sense to me (although, of course, if there is a God, he is free to make up whatever rules he wants . . .).

Without the rules of an established religion to live by, like most people, I make up my own. Sometimes that's a serious and demanding challenge; sometimes it's a licence to justify anything. I think of my parents' and my sisters' beliefs as being like houses that they've moved into (and which may require considerable alteration, renovation and extension). I'm slowly tacking together a shack of my own. It has follies and bizarre gothic facades alongside some stark functional sides. It's interesting to live in, but prone to collapse or to ridicule or to uncomfortable, damp nights. Sometimes, it can be exhilarating to abandon the shelter altogether and feel dizzily small and insignificant under the stars. Building it is difficult and life is short.

Margaret

I never particularly found it a burden to follow in the long line of my parents' spiritual inheritance. On the contrary, it was an inspiration and a blessing. I found myself at the age of sixteen with a deep inner faith in God, which, however, I found difficult to express. Rightly or wrongly, I felt my parents were good at relating to every other culture but not to my own. Deep down I had a growing awareness that, unlike my parents, my calling wasn't to other nations but to this nation. However, I felt very lacking in spirituality. I knew I was looking for something which would help me to live out my faith in a way that at least resembled what I read in the Bible, but I didn't know what it was.

Over the course of this spiritual search that summer I met a group of young people from Chichester who, I realized, had what I was looking for. They were full of fun, they were culturally relevant to normal people, but they had an enthusiasm for following Jesus which was confident and passionate. As an added bonus, within this group was a blond extrovert called Roger who definitely caught my eye! I went down to visit for the weekend and was taken to the first charismatic meeting of my life. I was awe-struck to hear people speaking in tongues and particularly to hear prophetic words. I felt that I was standing on holy ground and was too dumb-struck to know how to reach out and receive. Once I had overcome my sense of awe and complete unworthiness, I eventually asked Roger to pray for me too to be filled with the Holy Spirit. I believe this was the transformation I had unknowingly been searching for in my faith. From then on my walk with God was transformed.

At the end of that summer Roger and I started to go out together. Roger was a complete extrovert. As one of his friends said to him before he became a Christian, 'You are a born leader. The trouble is where you are leading everyone!'

However, now that he had become a Christian, he started leading to Christ his friends in the Rock Society which he had helped to found. They met as a youth group and then started to become filled with the Holy Spirit. This is when I came along. As the Holy Spirit met with us we rapidly became uninterested in going ice-skating or listening all night to records. We found it was much more exciting to worship God. In little crowded rooms we saw some amazing things happen. We would pray all night because we were enjoying it so much. Constantly new people were becoming Christians. Most of these people were inevitably friends from the same scene, many from a culture of music, drugs or different forms of the occult. The intensity of the worship meant that people with demonic problems spontaneously began to manifest it. I remember one night God convicted a teenage girl of the sin that she was involved in. She wouldn't repent. As a result, she was struck to the ground as stiff as a board, temporarily paralyzed. We had to carry her home. There was an incredible awareness of the imminence and awesomeness of God, as well as of the wonder of loving him.

We had no awareness of other churches like our own; we didn't know what we were doing. For myself, I drew on the foundations I had in God and then endeavoured to flow with what God was doing. We all read Scripture avidly to find answers to what we were seeing.

In those months we saw many young people saved, but lost a significant proportion due to lack of discipling. However, we grew to a core of about seventy committed Christians. In reality we had been a church for a long time before we dared to own that name. The name seemed to imply a maturity of years and wisdom which we felt we desperately lacked. We faced much opposition and criticism, but we knew, with an inward fire, that God was with us and was calling us to be somehow of significance for his kingdom in this nation. Eventually in 1983 we officially became a church. I was eighteen years old and Roger was twenty-four.

However, my family had bred in me not only a desire to lay down my life for God's kingdom, but also a great interest in education. I had become very ambitious to succeed academically. I worked hard and gained straight A grades in my 'A' Levels and a further Distinction and Merit in what were then called 'S' Levels. I was offered a place at Cambridge University to read History without being required to do the normal Oxbridge entrance exam. As soon as I heard this, I packed my bags at boarding school and was on the train down to Chichester. I knew I wanted to spend my 'gap year' there, growing in God and taking part in what he was doing there. This was soon after we had called ourselves a church.

This year between 'A' Levels and going to university was a foundational time for me spiritually. At key times over the years I have been aware that my sense of God's calling has been passed down through many generations. I have gained so much from that rich spiritual tradition. Their example has given me inspiration, vision, faith to shake a nation, and has led me to come to terms with the reality of self-sacrifice.

But in order to come into this inheritance I also had to cut some of the roots from my parents. This started with me deciding to be baptized as a believer, and was followed by chosing to stay in Chichester for the whole of my gap year instead of going to Malaysia. Both of these decisions caused some family traumas, but nothing like what was to come!

This must have been a challenging time for my parents. At that stage they had concerns about both the youthful and strongly charismatic nature of our emerging church. Yet, on the other hand, they wanted to do their best to encourage its evangelistic emphasis.

Before I went to Cambridge, Roger challenged me head-on, as only a bull in a china shop can do, as to what my reasons were for going. Was it part of God's calling for my life or was I just fulfilling my own ambition and following an expected cultural course? We had a steaming argument during which we both hurled Scriptures at each other. As a budding historian I was trained to argue. Several hours later I humbled myself and together we prayed and gave God the freedom to speak to me. So far he hadn't had a chance to get a word in edgeways! I had certainly met my match in Roger! Over the next few weeks as I prayed and fasted, I knew God said 'Go', but I knew there was no full-stop after the word 'Go'. That night I think the Spirit of God did major surgery on me. I had never been drunk on alcohol, but that night I was definitely drunk on something else! I lay for hours soaking in God's presence as if in a dream and felt completely intoxicated if I tried to get up.

Before I went off to Cambridge we got engaged. I knew without a shadow of doubt that Roger was the man for me. We loved each other with a passion, were tremendous friends and were both on fire for God. He burnt out his car visiting me in Cambridge, but it was a great year for me, full of stimulation academically and culturally. I asked Father God regularly if it was right for me to be there, and I felt at peace for the first year. Then that summer the affirmation from Heaven was removed. God spoke to us both independently and I knew it was time to come back to my primary calling.

To say it was traumatic for my parents would be a polite understatement. This time it was they who flung Scriptures at me and I don't blame them. I also knew that if I was to come back to Chichester there was no reason not to get married that very summer of 1985! I was longing for this and I wanted to throw the biggest party I could imagine at the thought that at last after four years together we could marry. But Mummy was in tears and it seemed that they weren't so confident of my choice of a partner as I was. The cultural gap was large and in my immaturity I hadn't known how to build the bridge. In addition, they hadn't had the benefit of seeing much of my life in Chichester.

It was the hardest thing I've ever done. I loved and respected them so deeply and yet somehow I knew I could find my spiritual inheritance only in obedience to God and not to them. However, whilst the process of the decision was painful, once they realized how serious we were they began to get behind the wedding preparations.

The wedding took the place of our Sunday meeting six weeks later and the whole church was invited. After we had danced our hearts out before God, Daddy stood before everyone and said they had 'every confidence that Roger was the right man for me'. It was a tribute to their flexibility.

In fact, I finished my degree in History at Bognor College (!) and later taught History at a secondary school in Chichester. But my 'real' job started straight after the wedding as we gave ourselves to pastoral work, teaching and doing whatever else was needed to lead the church. In 1986 we sent a team to plant a congregation in Bognor, in 1988 we planted in the north of Chichester. Over the next year we planted congregations in Bersted, Portsmouth City, Barnham and Selsey. During this time my parents have been very supportive, often advising us, acting as a reference point and speaking for us as a church on several occasions.

I remember vowing at a Leaders' Meeting that one thing I never wanted to do was to be working full-time as a teacher, be pregnant, and be the main leader of the mother congregation in Chichester all at the same time. Of course it happened!

In 1991 Chloe Elizabeth was born and then in 1994 a little boy called James. Graham Kendrick saw us with them at Spring Harvest this year, now aged a wonderful six years and three years. He commented, 'The youth church have children!' There are now about seven hundred church members and of course a diversity of ages. However, we feel a strong prophetic calling to recycle our church life to fit the emerging youth cultures. As a result we have also planted congregations that are not geographical but are related to youth culture. In addition, Roger has been involved with other people from around the country in launching a national movement called Remix which encourages and resources others in this similar vision to establish youth culture churches. At the ages of 37 and 32, Roger and I are now the Abrahams of Revelation Church and we are passionately cheering on our younger leaders.

We stand today as one church with its various cultural expressions in the different congregations. I know God called me as a missionary to this nation, but the dream comes full circle as we send out people into our own country and into other nations.

Ruth

On 16 July 1994, on a blazing hot summer's day, Greg and I were married. Not being part of a church which is licensed to marry, we had already 'done the legal bit' in the registry office a couple of days previously. So we were now free to decorate the local school hall and carry out our wedding ceremony in a style more true to ourselves. This allowed us, among other things, to write and say our own vows to one another.

One thing I was particularly keen to do was to make the 'giving the bride away' part more meaningful. Usually the vicar asks, 'Who gives the bride away?' and the father alone says, 'I do.' It all seems rather redundant. Although I had by that time already left home, I used this occasion as an opportunity to walk down the aisle with both my parents and to express my thanks to them for all that they had done for me. They replied by speaking of their love for me. I gather there was hardly a dry eye there, but what I remember most clearly was Dad talking about roots and wings.

Roots. There is no doubt that I have been given roots! Anyone who knows me, knows that I am firmly rooted in my family – and Greg has had to do battle with some of these roots on not a few occasions! They go deep down into a home upbringing of exceptional love and security. They also go deep down into a home centred around Jesus and a personal walk with him. They have born fruit in my love of nature and beauty, and in my appreciation of stillness and quiet – something my parents could never have imagined as I hit the Heavy Metal phase at the age of about fourteen! They can be seen in my deep passion for the Bible (even if I had not read it five times by the time I was fifteen like Dad!) and the way I love to talk and debate and discuss. They are demonstrated by my insistence in our home, with the young people we have living with us, that we all eat round the table together every evening rather than in front of the television. Greg sees a manifestation of my roots as I cycle along smiling with a wide open mouth, waving idiotically whenever I see him, looking just like Dad.

As I have read parts of this book and have listened to Mum as she has talked excitedly about all the historical research she is doing, I have become increasingly aware of the amazing spiritual heritage of which I am a part. I realize I owe so much of who I am and what I do to this. For example, I am very involved in the setting up of Fusion, the new national student initiative that Roger Ellis (my brother-in-law) is heading up. As I work on and pray into this I find it incredibly exciting to think that it was my great grandfather, Robert Wilder, who started interdenominational student ministry at a national level in Britain way back in 1892. What a heritage to be standing in!

I have also been very challenged and sobered as I have read about the work that Mum and Dad did in South East Asia, and about the thirty years of missionary service that my grandfather did in China: all the hardship and the suffering, the difficult working conditions and the long hours and just the sheer bravery and courage of what they did. I am increasingly challenged by the contrast between their lives and my secure upbringing in Stanstead Abbotts and present comfortable life in Chichester. As I read the stories I ask myself if I would be prepared to go through these things for Jesus. I have much to learn here.

Wings – what do they mean? Wings means being given freedom to discover who you are (remembering that we are ourselves only through our relationship with other people), to try out different expressions of yourself until you find the one that fits, and to explore for yourself who Jesus is and what part he is going to play in your life. As I hit my teens I had in front of me very well-known and respected Christian parents, a father with a particularly sharp mind, a brother who had been at Oxford and a sister who was at Cambridge and who was fast moving into Christian leadership. Wings were things I certainly needed to find!

Thanks to my older sister, who was always at the other end of the phone should Mum and Dad need advice, they managed to cope as I moved from one alternative scene to another (although I never lost my Christian faith). I remember one evening coming downstairs ready to go down to the pub, hair died black and back-combed, my make-up done heavily in black and purple in true gothic fashion. Mum looked at me in horror but said, 'Darling, your skirt picks out the colour of your eye-shadow so beautifully!'

My wings have actually been fairly easy to find. I owe this to understanding parents, Revelation Church, Greg and especially my elder sister who left the nest before me. In doing this she challenged some of the expectations and assumptions that our parents inevitably carried, so making it much easier for me to leave later on.

So now I lead a busy life! Having read Theology at Cambridge, I completed my master's degree from London Bible College, working at the same time as research assistant for Clive Calver, who was then the General Director of the Evangelical Alliance. I am now Head of Social Responsibility at the Evangelical Alliance and am a regular speaker at Spring Harvest. My desire is to see social justice as being at the centre of what it means to be a Christian, rather than an optional extra. I am also on the leadership team of Revelation Church and am starting to broaden my outside speaking ministry.

Greg and I try to keep our home open and welcoming and so always have people living with us. We want very much to get away from the privatized '2.4 family' mentality of much of our society and live lives that are much more inclusive. Often the traditional family home environment can seem difficult to penetrate for those on the outside, and churches can put it on a pedestal as the main aim in life in a way which does not help those who are single. Therefore, we have three people living with us, often young people who need a secure and supportive environment.

Greg heads up a justice and development organization called CRED. It runs a large education programme, raising young people's awareness of global justice issues, seeing on average twenty thousand pupils a year. We are also part of a fair-trade business. CRED is very involved in campaigning against western businesses which abuse the developing world, working in partnership with fashion designers to promote the just manufacturing of clothes. Overseas, we are particularly involved with a project in Ethiopia run by an outstanding woman called Jember Teferra. She runs an amazing work in four of the worst slums in Addis Ababa and is effecting real change.

Thus together we are trying to work out God's heart for the poor and the oppressed both overseas and also at home in the council estate that we live on. All of this means that Greg and I are very busy and have fun finding creative ways of spending time with each other. Our favourite is going away to a Bed and Breakfast for a night!

Mum and Dad have given me many ideals, even if they are expressed differently as I operate as a member of the next generation. I want to finish by quoting what I said to them on my wedding day:

To Martin and Elizabeth from Ruth

Mum and Dad, as I am about to marry Greg, I want to take this opportunity first to express my thanks to you both for all that you have done for me over the years.

As I look back and remember the good times we had as a family: the fun holidays all over the world, the picnics, walks and canoeing and the hours spent playing bezique and backgammon with you, Dad, I realize just how much you have imparted to me, from my deep appreciation of nature, beauty and stillness, to my hunger for and excitement over the Scriptures and all that God tells us about himself in them. Over the last few years I have become increasingly aware of the incredible spiritual heritage and blessings which I have received from both of you. And I want to thank you so much for the way that you have brought me up, and showed me by example what it means to have a close relationship with the living God. I thank you also for the way that you have prayed unceasingly for me every night as you go to bed.

As I have grown up, your love and unfailing commitment to me has provided the secure base that I needed. As I went through school, following behind my Oxbridge brother and sister, you never put any pressure on me – never expected me to be perfect, but always believed the best of me. In this way you have allowed me to develop my own character and be me, even if there have been a few hiccups on the way as you coped admirably with my black make-up and spiky hair and the alien boyfriends I brought home!

And so, as I move into this new chapter of my life, I am very aware of the secure foundation that I stand on because of you. Thank you. I love you both very much.

Epilogue

Our family saga continues. Through each of the generations each of us has faced the choice, 'What will I do with my life?' Despite the influence of our family heritage, we have each been free to develop our own personality. The biggest choice of all has been whether to love and serve God or not. In each generation one or two have chosen to go their own way, although the majority have walked in the spiritual footsteps of the family line. The missionary vision has gripped many of us, whether it has involved serving God in our homeland or overseas.

There is today a renewed sense of the importance of belonging to a family heritage. Many are rediscovering their historical roots. I and my children are deeply aware of the privilege of the line we have inherited and are now handing on to the next generation. As I recount our story I pray that my readers will rediscover all that is good in their past and pass on a God-centred heritage with a passion to make Christ known throughout the world.

Regarding the history of the missionary movement, much has happened in the 150 years since my great-grandparents sailed for India. Mission strategy has been hotly debated and has gradually evolved. Thousands of missionary recruits have gone out to all the corners of the earth, including many from All Nations Christian College. Through great suffering the church of God is now established in every nation. Yet there is still much work to be done before the Old Testament prophecy is fulfilled that 'The earth will be filled with the knowledge of the glory of God as the waters cover the sea' (Habakkuk 2:14).

One day Martin and I too will have to lay down our torch. As the next generation picks up the challenge, will my grandfather's dream at last come true –

The evangelization of the world in this generation?

Life's Tapestry
Martin Goldsmith Remembers
Martin Goldsmith

With humour and penetrating insight Martin Goldsmith shares anecdotes from his own life and ministry, and he encourages a new generation to live for Jesus Christ alone.

Goldsmith's time as a missionary with OMF and his present extensive, travelling ministry has given him the privilege of seeing God at work in various parts of the world including Indonesia, Malaysia, Africa, and Latin America. In this fascinating insight into the life of a missionary, evangelist and teacher, Martin Goldsmith looks back over forty years of Christian service and bequeaths a 'legacy' of a lifetime's experience.

"The joy of this book is that [Martin Goldsmith's] remarkable breadth of experience can be taken in. You'll laugh and cry, you'll be inspired and you'll be rebuked."
Margaret Ellis (from the foreword)

Martin Goldsmith is Associate Lecturer at All Nations Christian College and has a full-time speaking ministry that takes him throughout the world. Previously he served with OMF in Singapore, Malaysia, Indonesia and Thailand. As a Jewish Christian he is Vice President of The Church's Ministry among Jews and serves on the board of the European Jews for Jesus. He is the author of a number of books including *Islam and Christian Witness* (OM Publishing).

ISBN 1-85078-273-3

**OM
publishing**

God on the Move
Growth and Change in the Church Worldwide
Martin Goldsmith

What is God doing in the world today?

Martin Goldsmith provides succinct survey of the present state of the church worldwide demonstrating that while there are many areas of growth, an immense task still faces Christians. Many parts of Asia and Africa are responding to the gospel as never before, but secularsim continues to grow in the West.

"If you don't know how to share your faith with Jews, Muslims or ex-Atheists, then Martin Goldsmith's God on the Move *is for you . . . As renewal turns to revival, we must interface with the world God is wanting us to reach. This book helps us to do just that."*
Gerald Coates, Speaker, Author and Broadcaster.

"Few things are more encouraging for Christians than to know what God is doing throughout his world . . . Get the big picture as sketched here by Martin Goldsmith and so many more detailed pictures will make sense . . . This is not a book for the narrow-minded!"
Chris Wright, Principal, All Nations Christian College.

Martin Goldsmith is Associate Lecturer at All Nations Christian College and has a full-time speaking ministry that takes him throughout the world. Amongst his publications are *Islam and Christian Witness* **and** *Life's Tapestry*.

ISBN 1-85078-304-7

OM
publishing

God Can Be Trusted
God's Faithfulness to a child, wife and mother
Elizabeth Goldsmith

Brought up by missionary parents in China, and losing her mother during five year's separation by the war, Elizabeth Goldsmith's childhood years gave her many opportunities to see God's faithfulness in action.

Called to the mission field herself, her experiences as a missionary wife and mother in Indonesia tested her own personal faith many times.

ISBN 1-85078-243-1

OM
publishing

A Cracked Pot
Tales from the Heart of Life's Journey
Lizzy Wilson

Lizzy Wilson, an Irish midwife engaged in development work, takes us on a journey into the hearts and lives of people who are, for many different reasons, 'living separation' from those they love. With humour, warmth and great love of life and people, she shows the many ways in which a 'cracked pot', in the hands of its master creator, can make a difference in our hurting world with its kaleidoscope of needs.

These true short stories are based on Lizzy's experiences in many parts of the world, including war-torn Iraq, refugee Sudan, Australia, North Africa, and Ireland.

This book will have you laughing out loud and weeping with grief and frustration. It will make you call into question the modern Western emphasis on 'success' that has infiltrated even our thinking about Christian work, with the timely reminder that God asks rather for obedience and faithfulness.

"Here is someone who not only lives in the real world, but is more than able to communicate events, feelings and struggles of faith through vivid, memorable prose . . . I wish there were more books like this."
Adrian Plass.

"If you haven't time for an unputdownable book, don't read this one. I was completely drawn in . . . sharing in the joy and pain of women at the most vulnerable time of their lives. There's a searing reality, warmth and compassion born of Lizzy's own heart-break in this beautiful book which moved me to tears, yet made me rejoice. It's an experience I wouldn't have missed."
Michele Guinness.

Lizzy Wilson is a midwife currently engaged in Primary Healthcare in North Africa. She has worked in many parts of the world including Iraq, Australia, Ireland and the Sudan.

ISBN 1-85078-305-5

OM
publishing

A Flame of Sacred Love
The Life of Benjamin Broomhall, Friend of China
Norman Cliff

Benjamin Broomhall, brother-in-law of Hudson Taylor, was one of the best known Christian laymen in Britian in the latter part of the nineteenth century.

As the General Secretary of the China Inland Mission he was a prominent figure in churches and at large conventions where he spoke on China and the cause of missions. He was also well known by Cabinet Ministers and members of Parliament for his uncompromising stand against the evils of slavery and the opium trade, and in his lifetime he saw both evils largely eliminated.

Although he never set foot in China, Broomhall had a great influence on God's work in that land through the hundrds of young people he selected and sent out, including five of his own children.

"Behind many a Christian visionary stand those whose complementary gifts of steady wisdom and practical management, under God, enable the vision to be realised. Here is the engrossing story of a husband and wife partnership playing exactly such a role. In no small measure, it was Benjamin and Amelia Broomhall who enabled James Hudson Taylor's vision for the China Inland Mission to pass from dream to reality."
Rosemary Dowsett, OMF International, Conference and Training Ministry.

Norman Cliff is the great grandson of Benjamin Broomhall. He has researched and written about the history of missions in China in the nineteenth and twentieth centuries, including events during the Sino-Japanese War from 1937–1945. As a minister he had pastorates in South Africa and Zimbabwe. He is now in retirement in Haroldswood, Essex.

ISBN 1-85078-328-4

OM
publishing